Kenneth F. Dougherty, S.A., Ph.D., S.T.D.

General
ETHICS

An Introduction to the
Basic Principles of the Moral Life
According to St. Thomas Aquinas

*The study of morals since it treats of human acts
should consider first the general principles . . .*
  ST. THOMAS AQUINAS, *S. Theol.*
  P. I-II, q. 6, prologue.

GRAYMOOR PRESS, PEEKSKILL, NEW YORK
1959

By the same author:

Cosmology, 1st Edition, 1952

2nd Edition, 1953

3rd Edition, 1956
2nd Printing, 1959

Logic, 1956

Japanese Edition, University of Sophia Press, Tokyo, Japan, 1958

To

My Mother

In Memoriam

Mulier timens Dominum ipsa laudabitur.

Preface

THE AIM of *General Ethics* is to introduce the student to the basic concepts of morality knowable by natural reason. This presentation is Thomistic in doctrine and method taking into account the particular problems of morality in modern life. The need for new texts in Ethics is necessitated by the contingency of its matter. Whereas the fundamental principles of morality are constant throughout the ages, new and challenging moral problems arise. Man in the atomic age is the same essentially as man in ancient and medieval times. The ever changing circumstances of society, however, demand new applications of the fundamental moral principles.

The introduction of Moral Theology into the Catholic college curriculum has relieved the ethician of the burden of introducing parts of moral theology into the Ethics Course. This was formerly required in order that the student grasp the full import of moral principles in the present state of man. The Moral Theology Course now answers this need. The ethician concentrates on his proper domain: the natural foundation of morals. This is the aim of *General Ethics* as presented in this text. It is hoped that it will complement the Moral Theology Course in adequately informing the student of moral science.

Contents

Contents *continued*

PART THREE

LAW

Contents *continued*

A Critique of the Science of Ethics

I. DEFINITION OF ETHICS

A. NOMINAL DEFINITION. The nominal definition concerns the origin of a word and the manner in which it is used. The word "ethics" is derived from the Greek noun *ethike* which means moral virtue. The original root of the word is *ethos* which means customary ways of acting, habit or character.[1] The word "morals" also originates from the word for custom in the Latin noun *mos*. Custom becomes a second nature and produces an inclination similar to a natural one. When this takes place in the rational will in a habit of doing good, we speak of a moral virtue.[2]

Contemporary dictionary usage of the terms "ethics" and "morals" distinguishes between them. "Ethics" connotes the science of morals, while "morals" can refer not only to the science but also to the practice of morals. The word "ethics" was coined by the ancient Greeks, the chosen people of natural wisdom. It signified for them the rational inquiry into the principles of the moral life of man. This supposition of the term continues in the Christian era.

Words undergo changes in the things they stand for as we trace their history through the centuries. Although ethics is still

---

[1] Aristotle, *Nichomachean Ethics*, Bk. II, 1103a15.
[2] St. Thomas Aquinas, *Summa Theologica*, P. I-II, q. 58, a. 1.

called the science of morals, the term "science" is often used in a broad sense. Traditionally ethics meant a system of universal principles of morality with objective reference to the moral life of man. In contemporary usage ethics often means a history of ethical theories or a comparative study of morals in human history. No objectively certain universal principles are set forth. A survey of different and opposing ethical opinions are studied and one chooses what appears to be the best for oneself.[3]

This subjective attitude toward ethics can be traced largely to the influence of the German philosopher, Immanuel Kant (1724-1804). Kant maintained that man cannot know with objective certainty the essences of things and so in the moral sphere man cannot have a true science of the essential principles of morals. In practice Kant held that man must follow moral principles because they are useful even though he maintained they cannot be speculatively demonstrated. Kant has contributed greatly toward a liberal ethics of deed rather than creed.

This pragmatic view of ethics is accepted by many in our contemporary liberal society. In the pluralism of the American way of life it is found to be very convenient. Amidst a variety of religious beliefs and nationalistic backgrounds, it is found easier to communicate on the plane of good deeds. Ethics is often taken as a person's own private affair or point of view. In practice a certain ethical code is expected to be evidenced in business and politics, in the professions, in the home and school. More often the ethical code is determined by the will of the majority in a community. Walter Lippmann presents an objective analysis of this subjective standard of ethics in his work: *The Public Philosophy*.[4] Statistical surveys are commonly employed to indicate the mores of a community as if morality is to be judged by how many people favor a certain moral practice and how many condemn it.

In this text we use the term "ethics" to signify the science of morals in the strict sense of the term science. We shall study the implications of the science of ethics in our analysis of its subject matter, object and method. We approach ethics as the study of the moral life of man in the light of universal essential

[3] J. H. Melzer, *Philosophy in the Classroom*: A Report (Lincoln: University of Nebraska, 1954), pp. 55 ff.
[4] W. Lippmann, *The Public Philosophy* (N.Y.: Little Brown and Co., 1955).

principles of morality. These principles are founded on the objective nature of man.

As a science ethics first appeared in ancient Greece, especially in the philosophy of Plato and Aristotle. Although the Greeks were inferior to the ancient Hebrews in moral practices, the Greeks excelled all others in their scientific acumen. It is from this standpoint that we speak of them as the first ethicians. Ethics received a high development in the Christian era especially in the Scholastic Period in the Thirteenth Century.

A primary source of our text is the Nicomachean Ethics of Aristotle (B.C. 384-322). This ethical work is called Nicomachean because it was edited by Nicomachus, the son of Aristotle. The other primary sources are the works of St. Thomas Aquinas (1224/5-1274/5), especially his commentary on the ten books of the Ethics of Aristotle, those places of the Second Part of the *Summa Theologica* where he treats of ethical subjects, and the *Contra Gentiles*, Book Three. Opinions of contemporary ethicians are given and evaluated throughout the text.

B. THE REAL DEFINITION. Ethics is the practical normative science which by natural reason treats of human destiny and the rightness and wrongness of human acts. It is also called moral philosophy because it studies rationally the first principles of the moral life of man, the basic principles of the happy life as known by human reason.

Ethics is called a science because it terminates in certain knowledge of the moral life derived from principles known by natural reason. It investigates the reasons of moral rectitude and turpitude. The term "science" strictly connotes knowledge with certitude in the light of principles and causes. It is based on evidence known through intelligible principles. For example, when the ethician concludes that artificial birth control is wrong, he derives this conclusion from the natural law rationally evident to man.

Ethics is called a practical science rather than a speculative science because it is directed to action, to enable a person to live rightly. A speculative science has for its object the contemplation of truth as the science of metaphysics which studies being as being. Ethics endeavors to bring to its possessor the knowledge required by reason which is necessary for the moral life, the happy life. St. Thomas observes:

Moral philosophy is not for the contemplation of truth but it is for activity . . . that acquiring virtue we may be made good.[5]

Although ethics is a practical science, it is not an art. Art concerns the making of something such as the art of living happily. Ethics is concerned with the principles of the happy life, the knowledge of the principles directive of right conduct. The knowledge of the principles of the happy life is not the same as the art of living happily.

Ethics is a normative science because it studies the norms of right conduct. It investigates the moral principles according to which a person ought to live. In this inquiry one is not indulging in wishful thinking about an ideal world of what ought to be, a Utopia in the realm of the possible. Ethics is concerned with the human person existentially. It studies what the human person ought to be precisely as a human person.

C. THE SUBJECT-MATTER OF ETHICS. The subject matter of a science is what the science studies. Ethics studies man, the rational animal. We cannot speak of the ethics of animals or the ethics of atoms. We may speak of the ethics of horse-racing or the ethics of atomic warfare. Such subjects take their ethical value as they are related to man, the free, rational agent with rights and duties under God.

Man is the principal subject of ethics. There are many subsidiary subjects inasmuch as they involve human conduct, such as the ethics of business relations, politics, nuclear warfare. These subjects enter into the considerations of ethicians and the ethicians must be adequately informed concerning them. It is not enough that they know the principal subject, man.

Ethics shares its subject matter with other sciences. Man is also the subject of psychology, sociology, anthropology and other disciplines. Ethics is distinguished from all other sciences by the object that it seeks to render intelligible in its subject matter.

D. THE OBJECT OF ETHICS. The object of a science is that which distinguishes it from all other sciences. The object of ethics is human acts in their morality knowable by human reason. Morality is a property of human acts which is not physical like

[5] St. Thomas Aquinas, *In II Ethic.*, lect. 2, n. 256.

the property of shape or color. Morality is *sui generis* a property by reason of which a human act is good or evil as it conforms or does not conform to the moral law. It is the human act formally ordained to an end or goal. As St. Thomas says, moral philosophy considers "... the human act ordained to an end or man as he is voluntarily acting toward an end."[6]

The end after which we strive in our moral lives is either good or evil. It is what we ought to do or what we ought not to do as human persons. Ethics analyzes human conduct in the light of good and evil, right and duty, merit and demerit, divine law, natural law, positive law, conscience, obligation and sanction and the supreme destiny of man.

Psychology also considers human conduct and it is closely allied to ethics. On the clinical level this is evident. Mental disorders often involve moral disorders in the lives of people. Ethics depends on rational psychology for the demonstration that man is a rational animal, that he has a spiritual, immortal soul, that he is a free agent. These are demonstrable truths rather than undemonstrable postulates as Kant held.

The understanding of man as a rational animal is important to the ethician in his consideration of the morality of human acts. Man is not a spirit associated with an animal nature. He is substantially a rational animal, one being rather than two beings. Man is not two natures in association. His spiritual and animal powers are constituted in a substantial unity. The animal in man is subordinated naturally to the spiritual in the forming of the whole man. Man is not a spirit nor is man an animal; he is a rational animal. The proper understanding of man as a rational animal is important to a true ethics. Generally in contemporary life there is too much emphasis on man the animal.

Although psychology and ethics are closely associated, they are distinct. The object of ethics is the *human act* as conforming or not conforming with the moral law. The object of psychology is *the acts of man* as they conform or do not conform to the qualities proper to human nature in knowing, willing, instinctive behavior, and so forth.

Ethics is also closely allied to theodicy, the science of God in His existence, nature, and attributes. A proper understanding of God is basic to the study of man in his moral life. In

6 St. Thomas Aquinas, *In I Ethic.*, lect. 1, n. 3.

theodicy the existence of God, His nature and attributes are naturally demonstrated. These are not undemonstrable postulates of the practical reason as Kant affirmed. The natural intelligibility of God as the Creator and Destiny of nature, as the Author of the moral law, is basic to the intelligibility of the moral life of man. The banishment of God from the content of man's scientific knowledge always leads to the enthronement of the idol of the man-god. This engenders a pseudo-ethics of man as his own destiny under the guise of a benign humanism.

The existence of a personal God, the freedom of the human will and the immortality of the soul, are demonstrable truths basic to the proper establishment of the object of ethics. We shall come to understand this more fully in the development of the course. The morality of human acts is studied in Thomistic ethics as intelligible truth in the order of being.

D. THE METHOD OF ETHICS. The method of a science is the way in which it renders its object intelligible. It is the intellectual process by which it demonstrates its conclusions. Method and object are closely related as means to the end. The method of the practical science of ethics begins with the first principles of the practical reason. It deduces its conclusions from these first principles (i.e., do good and avoid evil). A first principle is called first because it is not deduced from another principle and is self-evident. The first principle is naturally known to all men, although it is not inborn. According to the natural disposition of knowing, it is immediately formulated. People may disagree and indeed there is a great deal of disagreement about what is good and what is evil but all men are aware in their human acts that good ought to be done and evil avoided.

The matter of ethics is drawn from experience. Knowledge begins with experience of our person, our body and the world around us. As St. Thomas says: ". . . the knowledge of moral matters is effected in this, that particular things are known."[7] The essential universal principle is derived from the individual contingent fact. The ethician must acquire the data of the moral life from experience. This does not mean of course that the ethician himself must be the subject of the virtues and the vices in order to know them. He can also induce the knowledge

---

[7] *In IV Ethic.,* lect. 15, n. 832.

of moral matters from the study of cases by observation and report.

In the light of the first principles of the practical reason formed in moral data the ethician deduces the proper principles of ethics. This method is both inductive and deductive.[8] It is inductive because it draws from the experience of the moral life. It is deductive because it descends from the first principles of the practical reason to the proper conclusions of the science of ethics. These proper principles are in the main the theses of the course.

What sort of certitude is obtained in the conclusions of ethics? By certitude is meant the firm assent to a truth based on motives that exclude prudent fear of error. Fear of error is excluded by motives which leave no room for reasonable doubt. The grounds for assent are reasonably sufficient. This is called formal certitude.

There are three kinds of formal certitude: metaphysical, physical and moral. Metaphysical certitude is founded on the essence of a thing. It is metaphysically certain that man is a rational animal. Physical certitude is founded on the physical law. It is physically certain that the earth moves in its orbit around the sun. Exceptions to physical certitude are possible by a miracle. Moral certitude has for its motive a moral law, such as parents ought to love their children. Normally parents do love their children. When parents act according to the norm of rational nature, they love their children. Exceptions, however, are possible. It must be noted that moral certitude is not probability. Certitude is graded according to firmness of assent which is more or less lacking in a probable judgment.

II. DIVISION OF ETHICS

Ethics is commonly divided into General Ethics and Special Ethics. General Ethics treats of the universal principles that govern human acts. Special Ethics applies these universal ethics to the chief forms of human conduct. These are treated in their main classes in the subdivisions of Individual and Social Ethics.

This text concerns General Ethics. It is divided into three parts: Part One: Human Destiny; Part Two: Human Conduct;

---

[8] *In IV Sent.,* d. 50, q. 1, a. 1.

and Part Three: Law. Part One is divided into three chapters: (I) Good and Evil; (II) The Ultimate Good: Man has a Final Destiny; (III) Man's Ultimate End is Happiness: The Possession of God. Part II (Human Conduct) is divided into five chapters: (I) The Analysis of the Human Act; (II) Voluntariness of the Human Act; (III) Involuntariness and Its Causes; (IV) Morality, the Standard of Human Conduct; (V) The Virtues. Part Three (Law) is divided into five chapters: (I) Law: The Obligation to Live Morally; (II) Conscience; (III) Obligation and Sanction; (IV) Crime and Punishment; (V) Right and Duty.

III. THE UTILITY OF ETHICS

Ethics is not studied as an introduction to morals. One studies mathematics in order that one might become mathematical but ethics presupposes morals in those who study its science. The unique benefit of moral philosophy is the acquisition of a philosophical insight into the moral order. The student is equipped with an understanding of the basic principles of morality in human life.

Higher education should impart a moral philosophy in the education of the whole person. A person is not fully educated unless he has studied the authentic vocation of the human person, the vocation of every person to the happy life and the moral means to achieve it, inasmuch as human reason can inform us of such things.

The collegiate period in a person's life is really a plastic period when ideals for life are formed. In the absence of a sound moral philosophy a pseudo-ethics can easily be formed. This sometimes springs from a lyricism of the arts, sentimentalized and romanticized as reverence for life, the search for the beautiful, or belief in man. Sometimes a pseudo-ethics is formed as a by-product of the physical sciences and technics. It appears as a crass pragmatism with a design for living based on utility, progress and material welfare.

The complexity of modern life involves a multitude of moral problems for man as an individual, and as a social being in the family and civic community. The daily newspaper is a constant reminder of the moral problems of our times in its reports of murder, theft, adultery, divorce, broken homes, juvenile delinquency, the rackets, and so on through the gamut of the vices. Modern journalism is of course in many ways a negative report of our times. The virtues are rarely extolled in the big city tabloids, as if such things do not make for popular human interest. The same may be said for the sophisticated theatre, the novel and the short story. Too often when these media attempt to be ethical, they adopt a "situational ethics," which constructs an "ethical principle" to fit a case. As an antidote to these decadent signs of the times, there is need for an objective understanding of ethical principles. There is too much intellectual sloth in this respect.

Modern man is in grave need of a return to basic moral principles. Higher education must take cognizance of this need because of the very nature of man as a moral being and also because of the widespread moral degradation. Although it cannot be maintained that knowledge is itself a moral virtue, moral practices do presuppose the knowledge of true moral principles. For the educated man and woman this should mean the possession of moral philosophy.

IV. ETHICS AND MORAL THEOLOGY

Morality is studied by ethics and moral theology. Ethics studies morality inasmuch as it can be known by human reason through man's own natural efforts. Moral theology extends beyond the natural to the supernatural moral order. It proceeds as a science by the light of faith and reason. All men are called to a supernatural destiny in the triune God: the Father, the Son and the Holy Spirit. This is achieved in the supernatural state of redemption in Christ. In the supernatural order there are more sublime precepts and counsels to live by, higher rights and duties, greater merits and demerits, a destiny in the intimate life of God.

A partial understanding of morality is given by ethics because it is limited to what is knowable by natural reason. For example, by the light of human reason man can know that God is the author of the natural law. But natural reason by its own power cannot know the triune God, the Author of revelation and grace. Ethics can inform man that artificial birth control is against nature. Moral theology informs man that artificial birth control is a mortal sin that deprives the soul of the life of grace and if unforgiven is punished in hell. Moral theology treats of sacred truths which surpass in dignity, complement in truth, and in no way contradict the principles of moral philosophy.

Although ethics gives a person a partial view of morality, it serves a definite purpose in the education of the whole man. Ethics is a philosophical science in its own right informing man of morality founded in human nature. The supernatural order does not contradict the natural; rather it complements and elevates the natural. Ethics demonstrates its own proper principles as a philosophical science. It does not take its principles from moral theology. Relative to moral theology, ethics in a certain way prepares the student for this higher study of morality by educating him in the understanding of the basic principles of morality founded in nature. The supernatural builds on the natural.

Suggested Reading

Aristotle, *Nicomachean Ethics*, Bk. I, Ch. 1-3. *

St. Thomas Aquinas, *In Ethicos*, Lib. I.

Cajetanus, *In I-II, Summa Theologica*.

J. Maritain, *Science and Wisdom* (London: Centenary Press, 1944)

"Ethics and Other Knowledge" in *Proceedings of The American Catholic Philosophical Association*, 1957, vol. XXXI, pp. 1-66.

Questions

1. Give the nominal definition of ethics. Cite some of the ways in which this term is used in modern times.

2. What is the real definition of ethics? Define the terms of the definition.

3. What is the principal subject of ethics? Cite some subsidiary subjects.

4. Specify the object of ethics. Discuss the object of ethics in relation to psychology and theodicy.

5. Is ethics a deductive, inductive or inductivo-deductive science? Explain your reply.

6. What kind of certitude is obtained in ethics? Compare this certitude with the other certitudes obtainable in the sciences.

7. What is meant by General Ethics? Special Ethics?

8. Write a short essay on the utility of ethics to you.

9. Discuss the relation of ethics and moral theology. Show that ethics is a science distinct from moral theology.

10. Identify some contemporary ethical problems.

---

*Quotations from Aristotle are taken from *The Works of Aristotle* edited by W. D. Ross (London: Oxford University Press, 1928).

Part One

Human Destiny

"God Is the Ultimate End of Things."
St. Thomas Aquinas
Contra Gentiles, Bk. III, Ch. XVIII.

INTRODUCTION

COLLEGIANS in their late teens and early twenties are forming ideals to live by. They are maturing in a design for living. One might call this period of life an intriguing adventure in human destiny. There is more to the vital queries that stir the human mind than the problems concerning a state in life, or the kind of work one would prefer in the arts or sciences, or in the areas of industry or commerce. There is the basic problem of human destiny, the authentic vocation of the human person in reality.

No person can escape this problem of human destiny. It is experienced in the constant "why?" of a questioning child, as he experiences the great, wide, wonderful world around him. It is the great question that haunts the mind of youth, as a man comes of age. It is the central theme amidst the responsibilities of adulthood and the reflections of old age. Men and women in all stages of life and in all walks of life have this problem in common. In simple terms it is the problem of happiness. It is the search for the meaning of human life.

Some of the finest pages of literature have been written on this vital concern of the human person. Men have earned the names of philosophers, "lovers of wisdom," because they have given to their fellow men some insight in what it means to be happy. St. Thomas Aquinas is outstanding among the philosophers for his clear and objective synthesis concerning the ultimate good of the human person. We base our study of this fundamental problem mainly on his writings in the *Summa Theologica,* the First Part of the Second Part, questions one to five.

Our study of Human Destiny is divided into three chapters: (I) Good and Evil; (II) The Ultimate Good: Man has a Final Destiny; (III) Man's Ultimate End is Happiness: the Possession of God.

CHAPTER ONE

Good and Evil

I. THE MEANING OF GOODNESS

As a prelude to the discussion of human destiny, it is necessary that we have clear and distinct objective concepts of what is meant by good and evil. Before we can establish that man is destined for the supreme good, the possession of happiness, we must first of all know what it means to be good. A little reflection shows that the term "good" is used in a variety of meanings. We may say that the young person's ideals are good or that this is a good-looking person or that he is good at making money.

Plato observes something common in what we call good. It is that which moves a person to action.

> And no one can deny that all percipient beings desire and hunt after good, and are eager to catch and have the good about them, and care not for the attainment of anything which is not accompanied by good.[1]

Experience testifies that action is born out of desire and desire is a motion of the will to a goal to be attained. The goal which is the end of seeking is called the good. The human person is capable of a multitude of desires which reach out for goods of many kinds. Some goods are real; other are only apparent. Man in his spiritual and animal life possesses a wide scope of

---

[1] Plato, *Philebus*, 20.

desires that extend from earth and heaven. Human life is a manifold pattern of spiritual and material *desires after spiritual and material* goods.

Aristotle defines the good as "That at which all things aim."[2] It is the end or goal of an action. When the goal is in some way proportionate to the nature of the being seeking it, when it perfects or completes the nature of the seeker in some way, it is really good for such a being. Healthy air, edible food, just wages are goods of man.

When we consider the good apart from the seeker or agent and consider it as that which is moving the agent to act, the good is considered as the end or goal. Aristotle defines the end as "that for the sake of which a thing is done."[3] The end is sought as a good or perfection of the agent.

Good and end are one and the same thing. The difference between them is only a mental distinction or a way of viewing the same thing from different points of study. For example, a worker labors for his wages and this is a good that perfects him in his needs. The wages are also his end or goal for working: that on account of which the work is done.

Good ——————— Wages ——————— End

| A perfection | That on account of |
| of the worker | which he works |

When we consider a person's estimate or judgment of the goodness of a thing, we consider its value. Value exists in a person and may or may not have real reference to things. When a person's evaluation of a thing corresponds to the objective goodness of a thing, it is a true value. When it does not correspond it is false.

There is a trend among some contemporary ethicians to consider the good merely from the standpoint of value, as if man's evaluation of a thing bestows goodness on it.

Edgar Sheffield Brightman, the Personalist philosopher, in the 1945 Fondren Lectures at Southern Methodist University interprets the good as value which exists only in a person.

---

[2] Aristotle, *Nicomachean Ethics*, Bk. I, Ch. 1, 1094a3.
[3] Aristotle, *Physics*, Bk. II, Ch. 3, 194b33.

Since value exists only in a person, a world of value could exist only in fully integrated persons in a well-ordered society.[4]

Value as a judgment of the good can exist only in a person judging but the good as real has a foundation in reality apart from the person judging. Healthy air is good for man whether man judges it to be so or fails to make a judgment about it. Honesty is good not because a fully integrated person in society judges it to be good. On the contrary, a person judges honesty to be good because it is objectively good. Brightman's view of the good is subjective, idealistic.

St. Thomas and all the Scholastic philosophers eschew a purely subjective evaluation of the good. The good is that at which all things aim. Why does man desire the good? It is because he is naturally moved toward the perfection, the fulfillment of his human nature. Human nature is the principle or source of human activity. Every created agent is incomplete, imperfect in some way. Man is drawn to act by the good proportionate to his human nature. "Every agent acts for an end."[5]

Whatever is good is naturally ordered to a nature. It is good for something. Apart from natural goods in the natural world, there are artificial goods in human society such as money, machines, the inventions of human ingenuity. These artificial goods are by the institution of man. They are good, however, only insofar as they complement or aid nature in some way. They are not given value purely by the creation of man. Money has value because it facilitates the exchange of goods in human society, which is natural to man as a social-rational animal. Machines are good because they facilitate works which are natural to man in his human needs. The good is what man seeks after according to his rational nature in the order of being.

II. THE KINDS OF GOODS

Ethics distinguishes three kinds of goods: the delectable, the useful and the perfective. The delectable good is the good

---

[4] E. S. Brightman, *Nature and Value* (N.Y.: Abingdon-Cokesbury Press, 1945), p. 85.
[5] *S. Theol.*, P. I-II, q. 1, a. 2, c.

that delights the appetite as when we speak of a good meal, a good-looking person. The useful good is the good that is sought as a means to an end, as a good tool, good money, a good machine. The perfective good is the good that conforms to rational nature, the moral good (*bonum honestum*).

A person may have delectable goods and useful goods and yet lack the perfective good. In other words a person may have good things that delight and are useful and yet not be a good person. It is only when the delectable and useful are ordered in the good life that they are perfective of man as man. If a person should live for what is delightful for its own sake or for utility for its own sake, he must fail as a human person. Rational nature in its natural inclinations toward proper ends as ordered by the Divine Intelligence must be the proximate norm of human acts. It is by the natural light of reason that man knows the perfective good.

> The perfective and the useful depend on accordance with reason, and consequently nothing is perfective or useful without being good. But the pleasant depends on agreement with the appetite, which tends sometimes to what is discordant with reason. Consequently not every object of pleasure is good in moral goodness which depends on the order of reason.[6]

St. Thomas explains: "... delight is the appetite's rest in the good possessed."[7] In man it pertains not only to the delight of the senses arising from the sensible goods such as good food, pleasant surroundings, but also to the rational will as it delights in the joys of life. Good music begets in man the pleasure of hearing pleasant sounds and also the joy in the rational will in appreciating the splendor of form of the beauty of music. The delights of conjugal love consist not only in the sensible delights of life together but also in the joys in the moral goodness of the virtues of fidelity, humility, patience and so forth in the common life of the home.

When a person lives as the plaything of his passions, his likes and dislikes, life becomes inhuman, disordered. It is no wonder that Jean Paul Sartre entitled one of his works *Nausea.* This is precisely the kind of life that the sensual life produces.

---

[6] S. *Theol.*, P. I-II, q. 34, a. 2, ad 1.
[7] S. *Theol.*, P. I-II, q. 2, a. 6, ad 1.

The pagan existentialist can offer no better way of life.

It is only when the delectable good conforms to rational nature that it can be perfective of the human person. This does not mean of course that the moral life must be a life of rigid reason without emotions. The conforming of the delectable to reason is not the same as the suppression of the delectable. There are two extremes to be avoided: on the one hand, the Puritanical extreme, the suppression of the delectable as such in life; on the other hand, the Hedonist extreme, the dominion of the delectable in life. The delectable is not necessarily evil nor is the delectable necessarily the perfective good.

Sometimes the perfective good is delectable as in the proper pleasures and joys of friendship and conjugal love. There are other instances when the perfective good is unpleasant. The parent, who rightfully punishes a disobedient child, causes the child displeasure. This can be a sorrowful task for the parent, although it is a perfective good.

The other class of goods, which are called the useful goods, must also be used as perfective goods of man. The useful good is the good that is sought as a means to an end.[8] For example, money is a useful good as a medium of exchange in human society. The useful good may or may not be delectable. Sometimes what is useful in the pursuit of proper ends is painful and even sorrowful. A great number of the human race earn their wages by the sweat of their brows in manual labor, which would not be undertaken were it not useful to their sustenance.

The useful good may or may not be perfective of man. Ever since the Industrial Revolution modern man has been especially enamored of utility and progress as though these were ends in themselves. This is crass utilitarianism. The present day emphasis on bigger and better production of material goods often seems to make utility the acme of goodness. Actually the useful goods are only means toward the fulfillment of the proper ends of man. The English social philosopher, Jeremy Bentham (1748-1833), is generally referred to as the philosopher of utilitarianism. Bentham has written much in the cause of altruism; however, his main theme is utility and progress. These must fail to give men a standard of proper values because the

[8] *S. Theol.*, P. I, q. 5, a. 6, ad 2.

moral standard has meaning only when it is founded on human nature under God.

Utilitarianism is one extreme which exaggerates the useful goods of man. The other extreme regards the useful material goods of the world as evil, for example, in the Manichean philosophy (named after Mani, third century Persian religious leader) and in contemporary so-called Christian Science. Brahmanism and other Oriental forms of idealistic monism regard the material goods of the world as illusory or unreal.[9] Christian Science also holds this denial of the material. Thomistic ethics views material and spiritual goods as useful goods of man as long as they are proportionate to the proper ends of human nature.

Everything that exists is good. St. Thomas explains: "Every creature partakes of goodness insofar as it partakes of the act of existence."[10] In three terse sentences St. Thomas summarizes his doctrine of the good.

> Everything is called good according to its perfection. Perfection in a thing is threefold: first, according to the constitution of its own being; secondly, in respect of any accidents being added as necessary for its perfect operation; thirdly, perfection consists in attaining to something else as end.[11]

Goodness is in the existential order. A man is good because he is a human being and possesses the powers and other qualities of human nature and because his human acts are conducted to proper goals. This latter consideration of the good is the proper object of ethics, the perfective or moral good of man. The delectable and useful goods of life are good for man inasmuch as they share in the perfective good of man.

III. THE MEANING OF EVIL

St. Thomas sums up the meaning of evil in the following passage:

> Evil imports the absence of good. But not every absence of good is evil. For absence of good can be taken in a

---

[9] An analysis of monism is given in *Cosmology* (Peekskill, Graymoor Press, 1956), p. 91 ff.
[10] *S. Theol.*, P. I-II, q. 18, a. 1.
[11] *Ibid.*, P. I, q. 6, a. 3.

privative and in a negative sense. Absence of good taken negatively is not evil; otherwise it would follow that what does not exist is evil, and also that everything would be evil, through not having the good belonging to something else; for instance, a man would be evil who had not the swiftness of the roe or the strength of the lion. But the absence of good taken in a privative sense is an evil; as for instance, the privation of sight (in man) is called blindness.[12]

Evil is defined as the lack of perfection in a subject to which it is due. As St. Thomas explains, evil is a privation and not merely a negation. It is not enough to say that evil is the absence of the good but rather that evil is the absence of a good or perfection in a subject to which it is due. It is not evil for man that he lacks the strength of the lion because such strength is not a perfection due to him.

Evil is a relative concept and can be understood only in relation to a subject deprived of a due perfection. We do not speak of chipped stones as wounded because a wound is only predicated as an evil of organisms. Or again, we do not speak of the bad morals of runaway horses because good or bad morals can only be attributed to persons.

Evil can be physical or moral. Physical evil is the privation of a physical perfection in a thing. Moral evil is the privation of a moral perfection in a person. Evil demands a subject or material cause, because evil is a privation, a lack of due perfection, and there must be something that lacks perfection. This is the only true causality that evil has as a survey of the four causes shows.

Material Cause: that from which a thing is made. Material in this context does not necessarily mean matter but rather subject. Evil requires a subject, which is deprived of some perfection. A liar is a person who has deliberately deprived himself of speaking truth.
Formal Cause: that in which a thing is constituted. Evil does not inform a subject or convey a perfection to a subject. Rather it deforms or deprives a perfection from a subject. A lie deforms a man in not acting as a man should for truth.
Efficient Cause: that by which a thing is made. Evil is not something positive since it is not produced as a per-

---

[12] *S. Theol.*, P. I, q. 43, a. 3.

fection in a subject. Rather it has a deficient cause which is a defect of an agent. The liar does not produce the truth that he should.

Final Cause: that on account of which a thing is made. Evil does not have a final cause since the good and the end are one and the same. There is an apparent good which may be the motive for a lie but this is not a true good or final cause.

People sometimes refer to good and evil as if they are not objective but only points of view. The politician who has lied and stolen from public funds certainly has many good things as the bounty for his cleverness. On the other hand, the public funds are deprived of what is due to them. From the point of view of the politician, he has gained good things. From the point of view of the public funds there is an evil committed. One might ask precisely how the politician has suffered the privation of evil? The fallacy in this reasoning is that the term good as gained by the politician is viewed from the aspect of the delectable and useful goods. Moral good and evil are judged according to the perfective good. The politician who lies and steals really deprives himself of truth and justice. The moral relations of truth and justice are as real as material relations. Moral deprivations are far worse for the human person than physical deprivation.

IV. EXAGGERATED OPTIMISM AND PESSIMISM

One can espouse extreme philosophies of good or evil. There are exaggerated optimist philosophies and pessimist philosophies. The exaggerated optimist does not give sufficient place to evil in his system. Gottfried von Leibnitz (1646-1716) affirmed that ours is the best possible world.[13] Leibnitz believed that our world is the best because God always does what is best. However, there is not sufficient reason for this assertion since the world is contingent. The world can be or not be. God, the Necessary Being, cannot be necessitated by what is contingent. Our world could be a better world. It is good for the purpose to which God ordains it.

---

[13] *Philosophical Works of Leibnitz*, edited by C. Gerhardt (7 vols., Berlin: 1875-90), Vol. 2, p. 424.

A far more prevailing trend is the pessimist philosophy. The term "pessimism" came into use from the time of Coleridge in the last century, although as a philosophy it can be traced to ancient times. It maintains that evil prevails in life. Usually associated with the fatalism of paganism, pessimism is also found in certain Protestant confessions, particularly in Calvinism and neo-Calvinism as in the beliefs of Karl Barth and Reinhold Niebuhr.

The Oriental philosophies abound in pessimistic outlooks. Brahmanism in the verses called Bhartrihari affirms:

> Man's life is limited to one hundred years: night takes up half of these; one half of the remainder is absorbed by infancy and old age; the rest is passed in the midst of the sicknesses, separations and adversities which accompany life . . .

There are definite strains of pessimism in Greek thought. Homer in the *Iliad* speaks of man as the most unhappy of all beings, and he adds that his lot is to live a life of woes. Euripides sees nothing in life but labor. In his work *The Desperate* he considers happiness to be like a deceitful phantom and death our liberator.

A desperate cry of anguish is heard in Europe again in the revival of paganism. One finds this trend in the lyricism of Byron, Baudelaire and Heine. It is principally in Arthur Schopenhauer (1788-1860) that modern pessimism takes form as a philosophy. "The end of life is not happiness," he wrote, "but rather work, deprivation, misery and suffering."[14]

In contemporary literature pessimism runs rampant. The plays of Jean Paul Sartre are an outstanding example of this trend in the West of the twentieth century. In his serious philosophical work, *On Being and Nothing*, Sartre considers life to be desperate, even absurd.[15] Man has no destiny; he is always desiring without rest. It has happened simply that existence was given to him and he chooses to live it. There are no fixed laws to govern him. Only by pursuing his existence on his own can he ever effectively mould his own nature.

---

[14] A. Schopenhauer, *The World as Will,* Supplement to the Fourth Book, Ch. 49.

[15] J. Sartre, *On Being and Nothing* (Paris: 1943). The best analysis of this work is to be found in G. Varet, *The Ontology of Sartre* (Paris: 1948).

Schopenhauer believed that ours is the worst possible world and Sartre finds it nauseating. The biography of the pessimist and the spirit of the times in which he lives is an important key toward understanding his philosophy. Schopenhauer had an unhappy childhood and youth. He was jealous of the success of his rival, Hegel. Sartre echoes the plaintive cry of many in France who cannot adjust to the economic and political plight of a once glorious nation. Philosophically the pessimist is confused as to what is real. He mistakes shadow for substance, evil for reality. Experience and reason affirm that human life is compounded of joys and sorrows. There are evils in life but life is not evil.

Man is naturally inclined to the good rather than evil. Moral as well as physical evil can be the occasion for moral goodness. Heroic acts of virtue are often born in the contest of good and evil. The carnal tempter can be the occasion of proved chastity in the virtuous. Charity to the poor, the sick, the unfortunate has given to human history some of its finest persons. The pessimist has given only his broodings and melancholy. The radical defect of pessimism is its failure to understand the meaning of human destiny, the problem with which we are concerned in the following chapters.

Suggested Reading

Aristotle, *Nicomachean Ethics*, Bk. I, ch. 4-12; Metaphysics, 1051a 4-21.

St. Thomas Aquinas, *On Truth*, Bk. I, Ch. I; S. *Theol.*, P. I, q. 6, a. 3; *Contra Gent.*, Bk. I, Ch. 37, *On Evil*, aa. 1, 2, 3; S. *Theol.*, P. I, q. 48, a. 3; *Contra Gent.*, Bk. III, Ch. 10.

E. Smith, *The Goodness of Being in Thomistic Philosophy and Its Contemporary Significance* (Washington, D.C.: Catholic Univ. Press, 1947).

Existentialism from Dostoyevsky to Sartre, Selected and Introduced by W. Kaufmann (N.Y.: Meridian, 1956).

Questions

1. Define the good according to Aristotle. Explain the definition.
2. What is meant by the subjective approach to the good? Illustrate this trend.
3. What is meant by the end? Are the end and the good the same thing? Explain your reply.

4. Define and illustrate what is meant by the perfective, delectable and useful good.

5. Cite two extreme views in the history of thought regarding the delectable good. The useful good.

6. Compare the perfective, delectable and useful good.

7. Cite the three ways given by St. Thomas in which every created being is called good.

8. Define evil. Explain the definition.

9. Discuss evil and the four causes.

10. Evaluate exaggerated optimism and pessimism.

11. Modern novels and plays often describe our present generation in a pessimistic manner. The main characters often look back on life with anger, forward with despair, around them with disgust and within with anguish. How do you explain the pessimistic trend of so many present day authors?

CHAPTER TWO

The Ultimate Good: Man Has a Final Destiny

I. The Problem.
II. Thesis I: Man Acts for an Ultimate End.
III. The Ultimate End Is One and the Same for All Men.

I. THE PROBLEM

THE PROBLEM of the ultimate end of man is the problem of human destiny. Is there a purpose to human life, which governs our lives, a journey's end to all the desires and strivings of the human person? Or is life merely a matter of chance, a mere plaything of fancy? If there is purpose in life, is it a man-made goal so that man is the maker of his own destiny? Or is man naturally ordained to a final destiny in the order of nature?

No matter how one estimates the problem of human destiny, everyone has experienced it in some way. Human destiny is not a problem that can wait for the musings of old age. Youth wants to know the answer as well as the more matured mind. Ethics serves a high purpose in the college curriculum in clearly identifying the problem of human destiny and answering it objectively according to natural reason. The collegian is interested in "making something out of life." This means more than preparing for a job, a profession or even a state in life. It concerns the authentic vocation of the human person.

The kind of answer given to this basic vital problem profoundly affects a person's life. A person who believes that nature is arbitrary to goals, that human destiny is the product of human ingenuity, will compose a man-made map of life. His dedication at best will be to man and man as he understands him. On the other hand, a person who believes that all nature is the creation of a personal God and that man is destined to be happy in the possession of God will be directed to live a life of dedication to God, the Supreme Good.

There are some persons who endeavor to dismiss any clear objective answers to the problem of human destiny. They maintain that man cannot know ultimates. One can at best compose myths about final destiny. Ethics for them is a workable standard of values for the goods of this world. Professor Harry A. Overstreet writes:

> Socrates gave no finished catalogue of the 'truths' of the world. He gave rather the impulse to search. This is far better, I feel, than dogmatic certainty. When we are aware there are glories of life still hidden from us, we walk humbly before the Great Unknown.[1]

Actually this is an agnostic outlook on life: the belief that man cannot be certain of the existence of a personal God, the Supreme Good, the ultimate end of man. Positively, however, the agnostic has belief in something as the master-value in life, a sort of made to order ultimate good. It is himself.

A person can subjectively devise the myth of a false ultimate good. One may attempt to follow man-made goals because they seem to work out in the situations of life. But this subjectivism is not in accord with reality. Thomistic ethics endeavors to demonstrate that man according to his rational nature acts for an ultimate end and that this is natural to him.

II. THESIS: MAN ACTS FOR AN ULTIMATE GOOD

I. EXPLANATION OF TERMS. By the ultimate good is meant the good or end that is last and beyond which nothing is sought because it gives the agent perfect satisfaction. It is the end of all ends. In the words of St. Thomas:

> The ultimate end of man bounds his natural desire so that when that is reached, nothing further is sought; for if there is still a tendency to something else, the end of rest is not yet gained.[2]

One may speak of an ultimate good in a relative or an absolute sense. A relatively ultimate good is ultimate only in

---

[1] *This I Believe,* edited by E. R. Murrow (London: Hamish Hamilton, 1953), "Professor Harry A. Overstreet," p. 171.
[2] *Contra Gent.,* Bk. III, Ch. 48.

respect to a certain series of acts. For example, relative to the college curriculum, graduation is ultimate. Graduation from college is not ultimate in respect to every human act. It may be the beginning of a new series of acts, such as entrance into medical school, the seminary, a position in business. The absolutely ultimate good is the last end for every human act. It completely satisfies the human person so that beyond it no other good is sought. It is the supreme good not only of man but of the whole order of being as metaphysics demonstrates.

In ethics our concern is with the ultimate good of man. Our concern is with the ultimate good or end of human acts. By a human act is meant an act done with deliberate knowledge. Such acts are to be distinguished from what the Scholastics call "acts of man" such as growth, digestion, dreams, all acts of man which are done without deliberate knowledge. It is our burden to prove that the human acts of man have an ultimate good which totally satisfies man.

This does not mean that a person is always actually intending the ultimate good in each and every human act. Man at least virtually intends the ultimate good. By a virtual intention is meant an intention which influences one's course of action, although one is not actually always adverting to it. For example, a man on his journey home does not actually intend his destination every step of the way. However, his intention to go home is influencing his acts en route.

II. OPPONENTS OF THE THESIS: All anti-finalists, who maintain that man is not naturally determined toward any fixed goal. Ever since Descartes (1596-1650), anti-finalism has prevailed in the modern school of thought.

A contemporary "naturalist appraisal" of human conduct which is adverse to naturally determined goals and especially the ultimate good is given by Professor Walter T. Stace of Princeton University in an article entitled "Man Against Darkness." Stace in his anti-finalism goes far beyond Descartes, who was a religious man.

> Since the world is not ruled by a spiritual being, but rather by blind forces, there cannot be any ideals, moral or otherwise, in the universe around us. Our ideals, there-

fore, must proceed from our own minds; they are our own inventions. Thus the world which surrounds us is nothing but an immense spiritual emptiness . . . purposeless, senseless, meaningless . . . the life of man is purposeless and meaningless too . . .[3]

III. SENSE OF THE THESIS: It is not the aim of the thesis to affirm that man acts for an end naturally. This is established in metaphysics in the thesis: "Every being acts for an end." The aim in this thesis is to conclude from rational grounds that man acts for an ultimate end naturally. Furthermore, the thesis does not concern the nature of the ultimate end but only that it exists. The following theses concern the identity of the ultimate end.

IV. PROOF OF THE THESIS: Man Acts for an Ultimate Good or End. In a dependent series of ends there must be an independent or absolutely ultimate end.

But man acts in a dependent series of ends.

Therefore, man acts for an absolutely ultimate end.

Proof of the Major. In a dependent series of ends, one end or goal depends upon another for its existence. But a series of dependent ends without an ultimate or independent end is repugnant to reason. A series of dependents demands the existence of an independent on which the others depend. Dependency implies independency as contingency implies necessity and imperfection implies perfection. It would be impossible to have a dependent series of ends without an independent or ultimate end which really explains the being of the series in its finality.

Proof of the Minor. Man acts in a dependent series of ends or goods. Human strivings are a series of means and ends. What we desire as an end today is the means to other ends in the future. There is no end in this mortal life that totally satisfies the human person. Our spirit is ever restless, striving, achieving only to strive again toward other goals. There is no perfect rest of the human person in any finite good or goods.

Therefore, man acts for an absolutely ultimate end or good. The very being of the imperfect, finite, dependent series of

---

[3] W. T. Stace, "Man Against Darkness," in *Atlantic Monthly* (Sept. 1948).

ends or goods demands the perfect, infinite, independent good, an ultimate end or good. Reason and reality demand that there be an ultimate good, a journey's end to life's desires, which is the ultimate perfection of man.

St. Thomas argues that there must be an ultimate good to explain with sufficient reason man's striving toward the good.

> That which is first in the order of intention is the principle as it were moving the appetite; consequently if you remove this principle there will be nothing to move the appetite. On the other hand, the principle in execution is that wherein operation has its beginning; and if this principle be taken away no one will begin to work. Now the principle in the intention is the last end; while the principle in execution is the first of the things which are ordained to the end. Consequently on neither side is it possible to go on to infinity; since if there were no last end, nothing would be desired nor would any agent have its term nor would the intention of the agent be at rest; while, if there is no first thing among those ordained to the end, none would begin to work at anything and counsel would have no term but would continue indefinitely.[4]

Thus St. Thomas argues that man is naturally moved to an ultimate end. He concludes that life is ultimately meaningful, purposeful. Aquinas was equipped with a sound metaphysics whereby he was able to answer the problem of man and the ultimate good. The anti-finalist, lacking a metaphysics, is not equipped to state and answer the problem objectively. It is no wonder that Professor Stace ends his quest with a confused view of life and that Sartre speaks of life as "a useless passion."

III. THE ULTIMATE GOOD IS ONE AND THE SAME FOR ALL MEN

A. THE ULTIMATE GOOD IS ONE. Can the ultimate good of man be composed of two or more goods which in their totality completely satisfy man? Some people live as if human destiny can be achieved in the possession of an abundance of the goods of this world. However, it is objectively impossible that the

---

[4] S. Theol., P. I-II, q. 1, a. 4.

ultimate good of man should be complex. The ultimate end must be one in being. St. Thomas explains:

> A man desires for his ultimate end that which he desires as his perfect and crowning good. . . . It is, therefore, necessary for the ultimate end so to fill man's appetite that nothing is left beside it for man to desire. This is not possible if something else be required for his perfection. Consequently it is not possible for the appetite so to tend to two things as though each were its perfect good.[5]

The ultimate good must perfectly satisfy man but man cannot be satisfied perfectly by a complex of goods. Either he possesses them in a series or all together. If he possesses them in a series as A then B then C, he will be desiring B and C when he only has A. Hence the series does not constitute perfect satisfaction. Neither can they perfectly satisfy if taken together at once because what can be composed can also be decomposed and so there is not perfect security. Perfect security is a characteristic of the perfect satisfaction of the ultimate good. No combination of goods can constitute the ultimate good of man. It can only be realized in an ultimate good, singular in being. B. THE ULTIMATE GOOD IS THE SAME FOR ALL MEN. All men are the same in species. They are rational animals. Men may differ accidentally according to color, nationality, culture, education, status in life, but all men share essentially the same nature. Human nature, the principle of activity in man, shares the same ultimate good with all created being. As a rational animal man shares with the pure spirits the ultimate good possessed as one's happiness.

Although the ultimate good is objectively the same for all men, subjectively it may sometimes differ from man to man. Our fallible human nature in this life can falsely identify created goods as if they can perfectly satisfy man. Some men live as if the purpose of life is merely to amass fortunes; others live as if life is a merry-go-round of good times, an adventure in self-indulgence.

Suggested Reading

Aristotle, *Nicomachean Ethics*, Bk. I, Ch. 4.

---

[5] *S. Theol.*, P. I-II, q. 1, a. 5.

St. Thomas Aquinas, *S. Theol.*, P. I II, qs. 1-7; *Contra Gent.* Bk. III, Ch. 17.

E. Gilson, *Moral Values and Moral Life, the System of St. Thomas Aquinas*, transl. by L. Ward (St. Louis: Herder, 1931).

Questions

1. State the problem of the ultimate good. Show its practical significance in our lives.
2. State the thesis on the ultimate good.
   a. Define the terms of the thesis.
   b. Who are the opponents?
   c. Give the sense of the thesis.
   d. Prove the thesis.
3. Is the ultimate good one in being or can it be many in a composition of goods such as the goods of fortune? Prove your reply.
4. State the reason why the ultimate good must be the same for all men. How do you reconcile this with the facts that some men differ from others in their estimation of human destiny?

CHAPTER THREE

The Ultimate Good of Man Is Happiness:

The Possession of God

I. Thesis II: The Ultimate Good of Man Is Happiness.
II. Thesis III: Happiness Is the Possession of God.
III. False Destinies.
IV. Aristotle and Human Destiny.
V. How Man Can Naturally Possess God,
Man's Ultimate Good.

AFTER IT IS ESTABLISHED that man is naturally destined for an ultimate good which is one and the same for all, the problem remains to identify the ultimate good of man. This is done according to the method of St. Thomas: to establish first that a thing exists and then to examine its nature. What is the essence of human destiny? In this chapter we shall undertake to answer this basic question of human life in the light of natural reason.

THESIS II:
The Ultimate Good of Man Is Happiness.

I. EXPLANATION OF TERMS. The ultimate good is the good that perfectly satisfies man and beyond which he does not strive. It may be considered from a threefold aspect: (1) as the good itself which is being sought (*finis qui*); (2) as the good possessed by the agent (*finis quo*); (3) as the good of an agent (*finis cui*). This thesis treats of the good as possessed by an agent or what it means to the agent to have the ultimate good. It is said that it gives man happiness.

St. Thomas explains that "Happiness is the perfect and sufficient good, it must needs set man's desire at rest and exclude every evil."[1] Our concern in this thesis is not with the imperfect happiness that man can obtain in life such as the happiness of one's state in life, happiness in marriage, in friendship. Human happiness in the proper sense consists in the possession of the ultimate good.

Every created being has one and the same ultimate good but only intelligent beings can possess the ultimate good as their happiness. Only pure spirits, the angels and the rational animal, man, can be destined for happiness. The inorganic world, and the vegetative and animal kingdoms lack the power to know the ultimate end as their ultimate end and to love its supreme goodness which is required of the happy state.

II. OPPONENTS OF THE THESIS: The antifinalists, the cynics and pessimists already cited who deny the ultimate end and perfect happiness of man.

III. SENSE OF THE THESIS: The thesis affirms that the ultimate end as possessed makes man happy in the perfect sense. All men seek happiness as their ultimate end (*beatitudo in communi*). The object of the thesis is not to determine the nature of the being which is the ultimate end. This is taken up in the following thesis.

IV. PROOF OF THE THESIS:

The ultimate good of man is the perfect good in which the rational will rests.
But the good in which the rational will rests is happiness.
Therefore, the ultimate good of man is happiness.

Proof of the major: The rational will rests in that which is the ultimate good of its natural motion. Otherwise it would not be ultimate but intermediate to a further good. There must be an ultimate good for man as was demonstrated in the first thesis.

Proof of the minor: The rational will does not rest in a good unless it is its perfect good. But the perfect good which sets man's desire at rest and which excludes every evil is happiness for man.

V. SCHOLION: Every Man Desires Happiness. Experience and

---

[1] S. *Theol.*, P. I-II, q. 5, a. 4.

reason testify that every man desires happiness. "For happiness is the perfect good that lulls the appetite altogether."[2] This is the supreme goal of life. It is naturally imprinted in the very being of man. Even the pessimist testifies to this truth. The frustrations of the pessimist are derived from an undue concern that man is meant for happiness amidst a troubled world where he cannot achieve it.

No man can be indifferent to happiness. It is not a good in the market of values that one can take or leave. Men have dreamed of utopias, ideal states of men in this world where happiness could be achieved. The Communists propose a classless society as if happiness can be achieved by removing the distinction of classes among men and equalizing the distribution of the goods of this world. They assume as all utopians that the finite goods of this world can satisfy the rational appetite for the universal perfect good. Actually the Communist experiment is a perversion of nature. Their dialectical materialism (Diamat) leaves man in a more wretched state of class conflict than it has found him.

THESIS III.

God Is the Happiness of Man.

It has been proved that man naturally is destined for an ultimate good, one and the same for all men, and that the possession of this ultimate good is happiness. Such a good cannot be identified with the imperfect goods of this world. In what being then is it to be found? It is asserted that God is the happiness of man.

1. EXPLANATION OF TERMS: By God is meant the Being Who is Pure Act, the Supreme Good, the First Cause and Ultimate End of all finite beings. He is Perfection Itself, the Plenitude of Being. By happiness is meant the ultimate good that satisfies man completely.

2. OPPONENTS: All who deny the reality of happiness as the perfect good that completely satisfies man, all who offer false destinies for man in the goods of this world.

Some philosophers have attempted to identify man's destiny

---

[2] S. Theol., P. I-II, q. 2, a. 8.

with the goods of the body as in the teachings of Aristippus, leader of the ancient Cyrenaic School in the fourth century, B.C. Contemporary literary trends often champion this hedonist design for living as in the novels of H. G. Wells, Sinclair Lewis, Somerset Maugham.

Others have attempted to identify human destiny with finite spiritual goods as the ancient Stoics, who identified happiness with human virtue, and Immanuel Kant, who believed that man's happiness consists in a good will.

Some philosophers have identified human destiny in the external material goods of life and the spiritual goods of fame and honor. The utilitarianism of Herbert Spencer and William James endeavored to find the happy life in the useful goods of this world. Progress and Plenty when used for human welfare are taken to mean happiness. The Marxist seeks human destiny in a classless society toward which he believes society is evolving and in which he believes man will be happy.

3. SENSE OF THE THESIS: By happiness is not meant a transitory happy act but rather a habitual state of happiness. Neither does it mean a happy condition such as man sometimes experiences in the passing joys of this life. The thesis asserts that the perfect satisfaction of man is in the ultimate end which is found in God.

4. PROOF: Happiness must be found in that which perfectly satisfies man.

But God, the Supreme Good, perfectly satisfies man.

Therefore, God is the happiness of man.

Proof of the major: From the definition of happiness it is evident that happiness is the possession of the perfect good that satisfies man. Otherwise we are not discussing happiness but some joyful state in life, which is obtained from the imperfect delectable goods. Man is only perfectly satisfied in happiness because he has reached his ultimate good, as was demonstrated in the preceding thesis.

Proof of the minor: God perfectly satisfies man because God is the Supreme Good.[3] In the plenitude of His Being He is All Good, the Good in which the goodness of every spiritual and corporeal good shares, as the fourth argument for the

---

[3] *S. Theol.*, P. I-II, q. 3, a. 8.

existence of God demonstrates. He is Truth Itself and so He satisfies the human intellect in its object, universal truth. He is Goodness Itself and so He satisfies the human will in its object, universal goodness. God is not a specifically good sort of being Who fits into one of the categories or grades of being. He is the All Good and the All True and fulfills the completion of truth and goodness after which man seeks.

5. SCHOLION: God Alone is The Happiness of Man. Man is destined to be happy in God alone since the ultimate end is one and the same for all men, as was shown. Furthermore, from the nature of God Himself, He must be one since He is Pure Act, devoid of potency which is the principle of division.[4] Polytheism is an absurd consequence of man's attempt to find his destiny in the goods of this world.

It is connatural to man to seek his destiny in God the Beginning and End of all things. Natural religion springs from this motion of man toward his ultimate end. It is found in some way in all people. Primitive tribes have their crude belief in "a high god."[5] There is a restlessness in the fallible nature of man in search of happiness. By reason of ignorance, decadent traditions, the follies of man, happiness is sometimes sought in false gods, false destinies. "Our hearts are restless, till they rest in Thee," St. Augustine wrote in his *Confessions*.[6]

III. FALSE DESTINIES

In search of his ultimate end, man sometimes invents myths which he superstitiously follows according to the pattern of a man-made religion. It is impossible to erase from the soul the search for the ultimate destiny of man. If one does not seek God, one invents false gods. The myths of the man-made gods did not end in the West with the polytheism of the ancient Greeks and Romans. The attempts of Mussolini to bring back the ancient gods of Imperial Rome and of Hitler to restore the German gods are two examples among many of twentieth century paganism. Perhaps the most widespread is the Soviet statolotry (state worship), the total dedication of man to the

---

[4] S. *Theol.*, P. I, q. 11, a. 3.
[5] Sieber-Muller, *The Social Life of Primitive Man* (Techny, Ill.: Mission Press, 1950), pp. 97, 99, 101.
[6] St. Augustine, *Confessions*, Bk. I, Ch. I.

deified Communist State. Theoretically the Communist denies that the State is the ultimate destiny of man. He seeks destiny in a classless society and believes that this will be achieved through the ruthless dictatorship of the proletariat.

> With the disappearance of classes the monopoly of education in every form will be abolished.... Under such circumstances the domination of man over man in any form becomes impossible and a great field will be opened for the social selection and the harmonious development of all the talents inherent in humanity....
> The development of the productive forces of the world communist society will make it possible to raise the well-being of the whole of humanity and to reduce to a minimum the time devoted to material production and consequently will enable culture to flourish as never before in history.[7]

This is the acme of human perfection according to the official Communist philosophy. It consists in material welfare in a classless society, an economic paradise. Human progress is measured solely in terms of material plenty, which it is believed will give rise to a great cultural esprit. As a trend of thought it is identified with the exaggerated concern of the nineteenth and twentieth century for material progress.

Karl Marx (1818-1883), the founder of the Communist philosophy, as he conceived it in his reflections in the British Museum at London, manifests the materialistic spirit of nineteenth century Europe. It was an age that looked to material welfare as the way to human progress and plenty. Adam Smith (1723-1790) in the opening words of *The Wealth of Nations*, an eighteenth century classic in the "science" of economics, wrote:

> The annual labor of every nation is the fund which originally supplies it with *all the necessaries and conveniences of life*....[8]

Jeremy Bentham (1784-1832), who may be justly termed the philosopher of the Economic Man, identified happiness and pleasure and considered the pleasant state of man a consequence

---

[7] *Program of the Communist International* (N.Y.: Workers Library Publishers, 1936), pp. 31, 32.
[8] A. Smith, *The Wealth of Nations* (New York: Random House, 1937), p. lvii.

of material well-being. John Stuart Mill sums up Bentham's Utility Principle in the following passage:

> The creed which accepts as the foundation of morals, Utility, or the Greatest Happiness Principle, holds that actions are right in proportion as they tend to promote happiness. By happiness is intended pleasure, and the absence of pain; by unhappiness, pain and the privation of pleasure.[9]

Bentham searches for happiness purely in man's world of achievement. Although Smith and Bentham have written many passages of high-sounding humanitarianism, it is difficult to envision a society rising out of such a philosophy which would be founded on objective moral standards under God, the ultimate end of man and source of the moral life. It is no wonder then that "the science" of economics became estranged to objective morality or attempted to be indifferent to it. The supply and demand principle of economic life was left open to interpretation in terms of the pleasure of man. Even when this is phrased in Bentham's appeal for the greatest pleasure for the greatest number of people, the interpretation is at best a utopian dream of materialistic altruism.

Swinburne has sung the praises of the Economic Man:

> Glory to man in the highest
> For man is the maker of things.

One cannot explain the rise of the Communist philosophy as dissociated from the age in which it was formed. It shares with the economic utilitarian philosophies of the last century a certain common ground of materialism. It is inspired by the same kind of roseate optimism in man's powers over nature. Frederick Engels, whom some regard as the cofounder with Marx of the Communist philosophy, wrote:

> Man, at last the master of his own form of social organization, becomes at the same time lord over Nature, his own master-free.[10]

Communism has deified the dictatorship of the working classes, which practically means the deification of the Praesidium

---

[9] J. S. Mill, *Utilitarianism* (London: J. M. Dent & Sons, Ltd., 1912), p. 6.
[10] F. Engels, *Socialism: Utopian and Scientific* (New York: International Publishers, 1935), p. 75.

or top men of the Soviet Union. The utilitarian philosophies of Bentham and writers of his like have deified the Economic Man in the captains of industry. Allied to this false destiny are other forms of worship of material goods such as the new cult of Aphrodite, the dedication of life to carnal pleasure. All agree on a finite god. In America the great protagonist of the pragmatic or utilitarian philosophy, William James (1842-1910) has noted: "I believe the only God worthy of the name must be finite."[11] Bertrand Russell, the very articulate materialist of our times, advises man to seek his destiny in Man alone:

> For in all things it is well to exalt the dignity of Man, by freeing him as far as possible from the tyranny of the non-human Power. (God)[12]

A strange variety of religious experiences has arisen in our times around the concept of the finite evolving god. It is the cult of the man-god, man in search of his ultimate destiny in himself, the maker of morals, the creator of new worlds. In the pluralism of contemporary society some openly profess this philosophy of life, as if man is an end in himself. In our fast-moving age the horizons of human conquest extend to the outer spaces in the world around us and new-found values replace the old in the world within us. It is important for all of us and especially for youth to understand the unchanging moral law that springs from the Unmoved First Mover and Creator of all. Unless we understand that our ultimate destiny cannot be founded in the finite but only in the Infinite Personal God, we can never hope to achieve our authentic vocation as a moral person.

St. Thomas explains that happiness is not to be looked for amongst the created goods of this world. It is to be found in our final destiny: God, He Who is All Truth and All Goodness.

> It is impossible for any created good to constitute man's happiness. For happiness is the perfect good which lulls the appetite altogether; else it would not be the last end, if something yet remained to be desired. Now the

---

[11] W. James, *Pluralistic Universe* (New York: Longmans, Green & Co., Inc., 1943), pp. 124-125.
[12] B. Russell, *Mysticism and Logic* (New York: Barnes & Noble, Inc., 1954), p. 46.

object of the will, i.e., man's appetite, is the universal good; just as the object of the intellect is the universal true. Hence it is evident that nothing can lull man's will but the universal good.[13]

The restlessness of our age, evident not only in so many personal lives but also in the mass culture of our society, is produced not simply by anxieties brought about by threats of atomic war, the actual horror of war, fears for economic security, the decline in home life and so on down the gamut of the evils of our age. Ultimately the anxieties and the restlessness are caused by the myths of false happiness, false destiny, false gods. Society and individuals can be ordered in goodness in the first place only when they are ordered to the Supreme Good in Whom all goods take their place and meaning in a total pattern for living that is true, purposeful, and meaningful.

IV. ARISTOTLE AND HUMAN DESTINY

Aristotle surpassed all the philosophers of the ancient world in his profound understanding of God as the first principle and the last end of all finite beings. It was common in the ancient Greek world to conceive of the gods not as first principles but as superior living powers who swayed the destinies of men from above. The first principles of things these philosophers believed were to be found in the physical elements that constitute the cosmos, in earth, air, fire, water. For Aristotle God is the first efficient cause and ultimate final cause of things.

In the Nicomachean Ethics Aristotle teaches that the highest activity of man is to contemplate the highest causes according to a divine power that is in man, the intellect.

> ... for man, therefore, the life according to reason is best and pleasantest, since reason more than anything else is man. This life, therefore is the happiest.[14]
> ... so does philosophic wisdom produce happiness; for being a part of virtue entire, by being possessed and actualizing itself, it makes a man happy.[15]

The happy life, therefore, for Aristotle is in the philosophic contemplation of God. This is emphasized in the Eudemian

---

[13] S. Theol. P. I-II, q. 2, a. 8.
[14] Nichomachean Ethics, 1177b30.
[15] Ibid., 1178 a 5-9; 1144a4.

Ethics where Aristotle stresses the ideal life in "the worship and contemplation of God."[16] This greatest of the Greek minds, however, had no certainty of personal immortality. For him the happy life is not in a life hereafter; it is in this life. It does not consist in a naturally perfect possession of the Ultimate Good because man in philosophic contemplation can know more and more about the highest causes.

St. Thomas and other great Scholastics present a more penetrating doctrine of the happiness of man as human destiny in the natural state.[17] The immortal soul contemplates God as the Author and End of nature in a permanent state of natural beatitude. This would take place in the after life of a naturally good soul. St. Thomas corrects and goes beyond Aristotle in this study. It is important that we keep in mind the limitations of Aristotle in his presentation of the happy life.

V. HOW MAN NATURALLY POSSESSES GOD, MAN'S ULTIMATE GOOD

Scholastic authors generally distinguish between formal and objective beatitude. By formal beatitude is meant the way in which man is constituted in happiness. By objective beatitude is meant the object that makes man happy. We have already demonstrated that God is man's objective beatitude. The problem of formal beatitude remains, namely, the way in which man is formally constituted in happiness. Is a man made happy by possessing God through the senses, or through the will, or through the intellect or through the will and the intellect?

It is evident that God cannot be possessed by the sense because the object of the senses must be corporeal and God is spiritual in the purest sense. We cannot see God with our bodily eyes nor can we feel Him in any sense experience. Union with God in happiness *is only possible by means* of the spiritual faculties of the soul. These spiritual faculties are both operative in the state of happiness that man attains. Man knows and enjoys God as his ultimate good.

Formal beatitude cannot be caused by the will because the

---

[16] *Eudemian Ethics*, 1249b20.
[17] W. O'Connor, *The Natural Desire For God* (Milwaukee: Marquette Univ. Press, 1948).

will has its object as possessed in love. Love presupposes knowledge. Man cannot love an object unless he first knows it. The soul must first of all be informed of its object before the will is moved to union. Hence it is primarily by the act of the intellect that man possesses his ultimate good.

Is it by the practical or speculative intellect that man possesses his ultimate good? It cannot be by the practical intellect because this phase of the intellect is ordered to some useful good as means to an end. But God is not the means to any end. He is the End of ends, the Ultimate End and Supreme Good. Consequently God is primarily possessed by the speculative phase of the intellect in contemplating God, for His own sake. This is the act of formal beatitude: the operation of the speculative intellect in contemplating God. St. Thomas explains:

> ...we desire to attain an intelligible end; we attain it through its being made present to us by an act of the intellect; and then the delighted will will rest in the end when attained.
> So therefore the essence of happiness consists in an act of the intellect but the delight that results from happiness pertains to the will.[18]

> Happiness consists in an operation of the speculative intellect rather than the practical.... It is evident from the fact that contemplation is sought principally for its own sake. But the act of the practical intellect is not sought for its own sake but for the sake of action: and these very actions are ordained to some end.[19]

This natural happiness is possible for man as the natural state is possible. Actually man is called to supernatural happiness in the vision and enjoyment of the triune God. In this sublime state God in his intimate life is our ultimate good, our happiness, formally possessed by the light of the beatific vision given to the speculative intellect.

Man in this life can have "...a certain participation of happiness by reason of a kind of enjoyment of the Sovereign Good."[20] "Men esteem that there is some kind of happiness to be had in this life, on account of a certain likeness to true

---

[18] S. Theol., P. I-II, q. 3, a. 4.
[19] Ibid., a. 5.
[20] S. Theol., P. I-II, q. 5, a. 3, ad 1.

happiness."[21] Life here on earth can be a way to happiness. On the part of nature, this means that the natural virtues be respected. The virtuous man in the perfective goodness of his life shares in some way naturally in the Supreme good, the Exemplar and Ultimate Good of all goods. This brings us to the question of the natural basis of the good life of man on earth. We shall consider this subject in Part Two: Human Conduct.

It is necessary to keep in mind the limitations of our inquiry. The complete insight into man the wayfarer on the way to his destiny is given in Christian Theology. Man elevated by grace and living according to the revealed truths of the Divine Saviour comes to his supernatural beatitude. The Christian philosopher in ethics studies man in his natural integrity. This partial study of man in his present condition is important as grace builds on nature.

Suggested Reading

Aristotle, *Nicomachean Ethics*, Bk. I, Chs. 5-12; Bk. X, Chs. 6 and 7.

St. Thomas Aquinas, *S. Theol.*, P. I II, q.2, aa. 1-8; q.3, aa. 3-8; q.5, aa. 5 and 8; *Contra Gent.*, Bk. III, Chs. 25-37.

W. Farrell, *A Companion to the Summa* (N.Y: Sheed and Ward, 1945) Vol. II, pp. 1-20.

E. Gilson, *Philosophy of St. Thomas Aquinas* (St. Louis: Herder Co., 1939), pp. 258-266.

Questions

1. Thesis: The Ultimate Good of Man is Happiness.
    a. Explain the terms of the thesis.
    b. Who are the opponents of the thesis?
    c. Prove the thesis.
2. How do you reconcile such commonplace statements as "I am supremely happy in my work." or "He has a perfectly happy marriage." with the assertion that happiness is only possessed in the attainment of the ultimate good?
3. Thesis: God is the Happiness of man.
    a. Explain the terms of the thesis.
    b. Who are the opponents of the thesis?
    c. Prove the thesis.
4. Discuss Aristotle's teaching on human destiny.
5. What is meant by formal beatitude? (a) How is beatitude possessed? (b) Give reasons for your reply.

[21] *S. Theol.*, P. I-II, q. 5, a. 3, ad 3.

6. How is the moral life related to the possession of the Ultimate Good?

7. Comment on the words of the Declaration of Independence: We hold these truths to be self-evident: That all men are created equal; that they are endowed by their Creator with certain un-alienable rights, that among these are life, liberty and the pursuit of happiness.

CONCLUSION TO PART ONE

Part One of *General Ethics* studies the ultimate good of man as known by natural reason. All morality is the movement of the rational creature toward its ultimate good, God. In the First Part of the Second Part of the *Summa Theologica* the Angelic Doctor considers this movement in general. The destiny of man is happiness, the possession of God.

Nature is a principle of morality so that man is naturally a moral agent. St. Thomas presents a masterful understanding of this fundamental principle of ethics and it is everywhere evidenced in his synthesis of the moral life. Morality is founded on the natural movement of man toward his ultimate good. In opposition to the Kantian trend which prevails in many contemporary ethical systems, Aquinas bases morality on nature as it is, rather than nature as it appears to be. Morality to be true must correspond to the real world rather than to points of view, a standard of man-made values.

Thomistic Ethics is eudaemonistic because it affirms that the supreme goal of life is happiness. It is to be distinguished from the hedonist teaching that human destiny is to be found in personal well-being. The happiness of which St. Thomas speaks is not a man-centered satisfaction. It is found in the contemplation of God. It is not a sensuous gratification but an intellectual vision of divine things that gives rest to the human spirit in its supreme destiny.

Thomistic Ethics is not an ethics simply for another world, so to speak, where man will contemplate God. It is also an ethics for this world because it informs man how to live according to nature. It directs human conduct according to law as found in nature and society under God. We shall explore these truths in Part II and III. It was necessary first of all to determine the supreme goal of life because the good and evil of human conduct naturally can only be ultimately judged in the light of human destiny.

Part Two

Human Conduct

"We must consider human acts in order to know by what acts we may attain happiness ..."

St. Thomas Aquinas
S. *Theol.*, P. I-II, q. 6, Prologue.

INTRODUCTION

AFTER CONSIDERING the ultimate good of man as it is known by reason, we now treat of the means toward acquiring the end. Part Two of *General Ethics* considers human conduct in the light of its moral goodness as productive of the good life which terminates in the happiness of possessing God insofar as human reason knows these truths. It comprises the study of human acts as St. Thomas treats them in the First Part of the Second Part of the *Summa Theologica*, questions six to forty-eight. This section is named "Human Conduct" because in present day English it connotes more clearly than the term "human acts" the general subject matter of this part of the course.

Part Two is divided into four chapters: (I) The Human Act (which considers its meaning, analysis and division into the elicited and commanded); (II) Voluntariness (which treats of the meaning of a voluntary act, its divisions and the principles of the double effect with particular application to our atomic age); (III) Involuntariness (its definition and causes); (IV) Morality (its meaning and the determinants of the morality of human acts).

The ethician's study of human conduct is by no means an academic hypothetical inquiry into the natural state of man. It is a highly important practical study which has direct bearing upon man in his present state called to a life in the grace of Christ. Once again we appeal to the principle that grace builds upon nature. Nature as such has no claim to grace but grace respects nature when it is given by God. It is important that the meaning of human conduct in its natural, moral constituents be objectively and clearly studied.

CHAPTER ONE

The Human Act

I. The Meaning of the Human Act.
II. The Analysis of the Human Act.
III. The Elicited and Commanded Acts.

I. THE MEANING OF THE HUMAN ACT

WHEN WE SPEAK of an act as human we mean that it is characteristic of man. It is an act that marks man for what he is, a rational, free agent, responsible for what he does, with rights and duties. It is a moral act, something that is intended by a person and which is either good or evil. St. Thomas explains:

> Those acts are properly called human which are voluntary because the will is the rational appetite, which is proper to man...[1]

Human acts are defined as acts done by man with knowledge and consent. They are deliberate acts, over which man has dominion. They comprise acts that either immediately or mediately proceed from the will illuminated by reason. Our deliberate thoughts and desires immediately are deliberate acts. External acts such as walking, talking, eating, drinking, kissing are mediately deliberate insofar as they proceed from members of the body moved by the will illumined by reason.

Whatever is done inadvertently as talking in one's sleep or whatever is done purely by nature, the natural functions of the body, as growth, digestion, are called "acts of man." They are distinguished from human acts. They take place in man but not by reason and consent. All unconscious acts in themselves belong to this class. The sources of compulsions, depressions or scrupulosity are sometimes to be found in the unconscious

---

[1] S. *Theol.*, P. I-II, q. 6, prologue.

as are some of the sources of dream material. Nowadays it has become fashionable in some circles to attribute most human frailties to the unconscious mind. This of course is erroneous and symptomatic of modern man's flight from responsibility.

Sometimes it is difficult to distinguish *human acts* from *acts of man*. In a court of law it must be decided whether a person charged with a crime really committed it deliberately or indeliberately out of ignorance or by force or by some other cause removing voluntariness from the act. Generally, however, we can distinguish the human acts from acts of man.

St. Thomas asserts that the human act is that which proceeds from a deliberate will "... not because the will itself deliberates but because it follows the deliberation of reason."[2] This deliberation of reason consists in the intellect knowing the end.

> It is essential to the voluntary act that its principle (the will) be within the agent together with some knowledge of the end.[3]

Both intellect and will contribute to the human act but in different ways. The intellect informs us of an end, something to be sought. The will tends to it inasmuch as it is a good to be sought. We do not love a person unless we first of all know a person and his characteristics. Reason concurs formally in the human act, the will materially. The will does not move until the person is first of all informed of something to be sought. The reaction of the will depends on the action of the intellect. Nothing is willed unless it is foreknown. The human act is not merely a voluntary act nor an intellectual act; it is an act that proceeds formally from the intellect and materially from the will. Materially in this context means that the voluntary act does not inform itself as to its end but receives its information of the end from the intellect.

This is a fundamental principle of Thomistic ethics. A human act can never possess its integral perfection simply by considering the will by itself or the intellect by itself. The perfection of the human act must involve the intellect and the will. This means that man must be correctly informed as to what

---

[2] *In II Sent.*, dist. 40, q. 1, a. 5.
[3] *S. Theol.*, P. I-II, q. 6, a. 2.

are the ends proper to his acts and his will must be disciplined to follow these ends.

Education of the intellect alone can never mean the education of the whole person in human conduct. The will must also be disciplined. The failure of the progressive education of John Dewey is largely due to his failure to appreciate the perfection of human acts. The free exchange of ideas as such is no more the perfection of the human act than is an excessive authoritarian training of the will without reason.

II. THE ANALYSIS OF THE INTEGRITY OF THE PERFECT HUMAN ACT

St. Thomas analyzes the various steps in the integrity of the human act in achieving its end. The act that achieves its end or goal is said to be perfect. He traces the steps from the comprehension of an object to the joy of achieving it. He lists twelve particular motions, six on the part of the intellect and six corresponding motions on the part of the will.[4]

On the Part of the Intellect

1. Simple apprehension of an object.
3. A judgment proposing to possess it.

5. Counsel: an inquiry as to the possible means required to possess the end.

7. The discretive judgment judges the means more suitable for acquiring the end.
9. Command of reason orders the will to carry out what it has accepted as the means to the end.
11. Knowledge of the possession of the good.

On the Part of the Will

2. Simple wish for it as a good.
4. Intention: a motion of the will to the object as a good.

6. Consent: an act of the will approving these means to the end proposed by reason.
8. Choice accepts a means in preference to the other means proposed as suitable to acquire the end.
10. The active use of the means to the end is undertaken by the will.

12. The joy of possession.

Three of these motions of the will—wish, intention and joy and their corresponding motions on the part of the intellect— pertain to the end. Three pertain to the means—consent, choice

[4] S. *Theol.*, P. I-II, q. 8, prologue.

and use—as do their correspondent mental motions. A human act is called imperfect when it does not go beyond intention because the means for executing the intention is not acquired. The integrity of the perfect human act requires that we intend some end and having chosen and used the apt means, enjoy its attainment.

The human act proceeds from the intellect and the will. Consequently in outlining the integrity of the perfect human act we should not consider the twelve motions cited as if all are independent isolated functions but rather as mutually related in constituting the perfection of the human act. The human act properly begins with the deliberate or proposed intention. The simple apprehension and simple wish is but a prelude necessary to judgment and intention. Reflection on our experience sometimes presents difficulties in distinguishing these various motions of intellect and will because of the speed with which they take place. This is true in many of our practical everyday experiences of intention, consent, choice, active use, and joy. At other times there may be a difference of years between intention of a goal and consent to the apt means and their use in acquiring the end as in extended business transactions, in choosing a state in life, or in marital proposals and consent.

III. ELICITED AND COMMANDED ACTS

We must now consider the different acts of the will; in the first place, those acts which belong to the will immediately as being elicited by the will; secondly, those acts which are commanded by the will.[5]

Every human act is an act elicited by the will with knowledge of the end. When the will moves another power of man to do something, this is called a commanded act, as when we will to move our bodily parts in walking or arousing a bodily passion such as anger. One may elicit an intention, a consent, or a choice to do something, and then the will moves the other powers to execute it as the will to go to the library to read the *Summa* of St. Thomas.

Experience testifies that our will commands other faculties of our human nature to execute certain things that we want

5 *S. Theol.,* P. I-II, q. 8, prologue.

done. The will is not alone in this, since the command is proposed by the intellect. This is what St. Thomas means when he says:

Command is an act of reason presupposing an act of the will in virtue of which the reason by its command moves (a lower power) to the execution of the act.[6]

A command is a declaration of the reason as when it is asserted: "Do this." or "This must be done." But the first mover of the soul in doing anything is the will. The reason moves in commanding only by the power of the will. This command of the will extends to the following powers in man:[7]

Commanded Acts

Soul

Acts of the will itself—to command oneself to will something as to study this evening. The exception is the first act of the will—happiness in common, which is a necessary act of the will.

Intellectual acts—to will to reason about something as the moral problems of one's state in life. The exceptions are the first principles and self-evident truths to which assent must be given.

Body

Sensitive powers—these are only partly subject to the command of the will and reason because they also have their own bodily dispositions such as evidenced in motility (muscular tonus and speed of movement), vitality or energy out-put—some people can work all day without tiring.

External acts of the body such as walking, talking, kissing, can be called commanded acts inasmuch as these external acts are moved by the sensitive powers and the latter are controllable by will and reason.[7]

----

[6] S. *Theol.*, P. I-II, q. 17, a. 1.
[7] S. *Theol.*, P. I-II, q. 17, a. 1-9.

Vegetative powers as growth and nutrition are not subject to the command of will and reason. We cannot command our growth.

As we ascend from the lower powers to the higher in man the command of will and reason increases. Man does not possess complete control over all the functions of his being. There are natural movements which follow from his nature and which are not subject to him as acts commanded by the human person. St. Thomas explains:

> That man lusts, although he wills not to lust, is due to a disposition of the body, whereby the sensitive appetite is hindered from perfect compliance with the command of reason.[8]

Freudians have made a great deal of the natural movements of man in reference to sex so that it would appear that sex is in command of man rather than man in command of sex. Sexual functions involve bodily dispositions in the male and female but the general functions of sex can be controlled normally by the commanded acts of the will and reason.

The Franciscan scientist Agostino Gemelli has carefully pointed out that pyschoanalysts today no longer make sexual instinct the central point of their teaching and also that Freud did not hold that sex is of supreme importance. However, Freud did exaggerate the role of libido or the motive energy of the sexual instinct and he fails to understand the true role of intellect and will as faculties of the spiritual soul in ordering life to its goals.[9]

Suggested Reading

Aristotle, *Nicomachean Ethics*, Bk. III, Chs. 1-5.

St. Thomas Aquinas, S. Theol., P. I-II, q. 6, as. 1-3; q. 8, as. 1-3; qs. 10-16; q. 17, as. 1-9.

W. Farrell, *A Companion to the Summa, op. cit.*, Vol. II, chs. 2, 3.

Questions

1. a. What is a human act?
   b. How is it distinguished from an act of man?

---

[8] *S. Theol.*, P. I-II, q. 17, a. 7, ad 1.
[9] A. Gemelli, *Psychoanalysis Today* translated by J. Chapin (New York: Kenedy and Sons, 1955), pp. 21 and ff.

2. What is the role of the intellect and the will in a human act?

3. With the aid of the diagram of the twelve steps in the integrity of the human act illustrate each step by examples from experience.

4. Define and illustrate an elicited act.

5. Define a commanded act.

6. Cite the various commanded acts and their exceptions.

7. What is the failure by excess of the Freudians in considering sex and human acts?

CHAPTER TWO

Voluntariness of the Human Act

I. MEANING OF VOLUNTARINESS

OUR STUDY of the human act made it clear that **voluntariness is of the essence of a human act. Every human act must** proceed from the will, the rational appetite. The voluntary act must be knowingly willed since a person must be informed of an object before he seeks it as a good. This does not necessarily mean that a person must here and now actually intend what he is doing. Voluntariness means more than actual intention. It also applies to virtual intentions. We shall study each of these kinds of intentions.

A virtual intention is an intention made in the past and which continues to influence the act that is being done, although a person is not actually aware of it while performing the act. The term "virtual" is derived from *virtus* in Latin meaning "power." By its power this kind of intention influences an act. A man travelling to Washington from New York by car is not *actually intending* his destination throughout his journey. His intention is virtual. It is influencing his acts so that he is directed toward Washington but it is not ever present to him. He may actually refer to Washington as his destination along the way but his acts for the most part are fixed on the proximate means that lead to his goal. In our study of man being drawn to his ultimate good, we said that the ultimate good is sometimes only virtually intended in this life. Such acts are voluntary.

As a consequence of the voluntariness of an act, it is imputable to an agent. Imputability means an act is morally attributed to a person as an act done with knowledge and consent. A person is responsible for such acts. Responsibility for an evil act is called guilt.

II. DIVISION OF VOLUNTARY ACTS

A. PERFECT AND IMPERFECT VOLUNTARY ACTS. A perfect voluntary act is an act done with knowledge of the end as an end and the relationship of means to end. This does not mean that one has such knowledge of the end that he knows everything about it. Perfect knowledge means that one knows what one is doing as to the end of the act and the relationship of means to end. One may not know the name of a gun, its caliber, range and so forth. The fact that one knows a gun can kill or inflict harm on others is sufficient for guilt, if one uses it without sufficient reason against another.

An imperfect voluntary act is an act done with imperfect knowledge of the end. St. Thomas explains:

> ... imperfect knowledge of the end consists in mere apprehension of the end without knowing it under the aspect of the end or the relationship of the means to that end.[1]

A bottle marked *As* would not be known by a layman to be arsenic, a very poisonous substance, and so one would not know that it is a means to kill. If the bottle is in a chemist's laboratory, a layman ordinarily would know that chemicals in general should only be used under the direction of competent people. However, in other circumstances he might use it out of sheer ignorance of its real content. There are varying degrees of imperfect voluntary acts caused by several modifiers. We shall study these in the following chapter.

---

[1] *S. Theol.*, P. I-II, q. 6, a. 2.

B. NECESSARY AND FREE VOLUNTARY ACTS. A voluntary act is free when it proceeds from the will with an indifferent judgment and with the power to do the opposite, e.g., to study; one may do so or not do so.[2] A voluntary act is necessary when it proceeds from the will with a judgment determined to one thing and so without a power to do the opposite. "The ultimate end moves the will necessarily because it is the perfect good."[3] Every voluntary act therefore is not free, although generally speaking the voluntary acts are free.

C. POSITIVE AND NEGATIVE VOLUNTARY ACTS. A positive voluntary act is an act that proceeds from the will through a real influence so that it is elicited or commanded: an elicited act of the love of God, the commanded act to eat nourishing food. A negative voluntary act depends on the will through the omission of an act that should be done—such as to omit deliberately to know the traffic regulations. There are an indefinite number of things that can be said to be omitted when one chooses something else to do. A negative voluntary act, however, always pertains to the deliberate omission of what one ought to do. There is a difference between not willing to do something and willing not to do what it is our duty to perform.

D. THE VOLUNTARY ACT IN ITSELF AND AS A CAUSE. An act is said to be voluntary in itself when it is intended as an end in itself or as a means to an end, as when a soldier intends to kill an enemy or fires his carbine with intention to kill. An act is voluntary in cause when it is unintended in itself but is a foreseen consequence of something that is intended in itself, as when a soldier in firing at the enemy foresees that he will shoot some innocent civilians who are nearby. The agent does not will the latter as an end or a means but knows that it is a consequence of his action. When the action intended is good and there is sufficient reason for it in the effect intended and the other effect is evil but an unavoidable byproduct of the act, the action is permitted. If, however, the act intended is itself evil, it cannot be allowed even if a good effect should follow— for example, to procure an abortion directly in order to save the woman's life.

---

[2] *S. Theol.*, P. I-II, q. 6, a. 2, ad 2.
[3] *Ibid.*, q. 10, a. 2, ad 3.

III. THE PRINCIPLE OF THE TWOFOLD EFFECT

A. PROBLEM. A more thorough study must be made of acts that are voluntary in cause or indirect voluntary acts as they are sometimes called. They occur very often in practical life and pose special problems in morals. Sometimes our human acts produce more than one consequence. We intend to do something that is good but its consequences are both good and evil. Practical life is not lived on an ideal plane and we often experience the difficulty of carrying out some good work because it will produce varied effects which will not all be good. Persons in authority—parents, teachers, civic officials—have to solve many problems of this kind as all of us do in our personal lives.

B. SOLUTION. The ethical principle of the twofold effect is given to solve such difficulties. It is permitted to perform an act, although a foreseen evil effect follows provided that:

1. The act is good *in itself* or at least indifferent;
2. its immediate effect is good;
3. the intention of the agent is good;
4. the agent has a proportionately grave reason for acting.

1. As regards the act itself that we intend to perform, it must be good in itself or at least indifferent. One may never perform acts that are evil in themselves such as lying or stealing, even though good effects are expected to be caused by them. An easy way to discover whether the act is good or at least indifferent in itself is to ask whether one has a right to it. One might question the moral goodness of operating a theater for legitimate entertainment since people may use such a place for illicit carnal pleasures. One has the right to operate a theater for legitimate entertainment when one has proper title to it and so the act is good in itself.

2. The good effect of the act must be immediate in the order of causality. In other words the good effect must not be obtained by means of the evil effect. Both good and evil effects can follow with equal immediacy. For example, the removal of a cancerous uterus of a pregnant woman has the immediate effects of saving a woman's life (good effect) and the death of the foetus (evil effect). They follow with equal

immediacy, but the good effect is not produced through the evil effect of the death of the child. The death of the child does not save the woman's life but rather the curative act or operation saves her life. The case is different when the death of a child is directly effected in an abortion so that the mother's life may be spared. The direct killing of the child is the means for saving the mother. The relation of the evil effect must not be as a means to the good effect.

Diagram:

1. Permitted: *Good Act* ⟶ good effect
   Given the good ↘ evil effect
   intent of the agent
   and a proportionately
   grave cause for permitting
   the evil.

2. Permitted: *Good Act* good effect
   Given the good
   intention of the agent evil effect
   and a proportionately
   grave cause for permitting
   the evil.

3. Never Permitted: *Good Act* ⟶ evil effect
   ↘ good effect

3. The agent must have a good intention. The evil effect must not be willed in itself but only permitted. One may render an otherwise licit act evil by a bad intention, as in the case of a doctor who removes a cancerous uterus and directly wills rather than permits the effect of sterility.

4. There must be a proportionately grave cause for permitting the evil effect. The good effect must be sufficiently good to compensate for allowing the evil effect. A greater good is required to compensate for permitting a morally evil effect by another than for a physically evil effect. A greater good is required when an evil effect is certain to follow than when it is only probable. A greater good is needed when the evil effect is injurious to the common good than if it is merely injurious to the individual's good.

A person being drafted into the armed service effects a good service to his country but at the same time he is exposing himself to certain moral dangers of the military life. The action of entering the military service for the protection of the nation is itself good, the good effect is not obtained by way of the evil effect, the intention of the agent is good (to serve his time in the cause of national defense), and there is a proportionately grave cause for his entry into the military life: the law of the nation for the common defense.

A young lady accepts a date from a young man for the senior prom. The date in effect means that she has a partner for the prom but it also means that she is dating a youth who she knows probably will insist that she attend an all night spree in the city. She is not certain what this will involve. However, her intentions are good. The act of dating is not evil in itself and the certainty of a partner at the senior prom is a good effect, but the all night spree would be a morally bad effect. There is not sufficient reason for exposing oneself to such dangers.

Cases. Apply the principles of the double effect to the following:

1. A pilot trapped in a burning plane is certain that he will be burned to death. He decides to shoot himself to spare himself the agony of being burned alive.

2. A prisoner shooting his way out of prison forces a guard to act as a shield against the fire of the other guards. May the captive guard be shot in preventing the prisoner's escape?

3. A mother exposes herself to probable death in rescuing her child from a burning building.

4. A stock car racer risks his life for a large cash prize in a race gravely dangerous to life and limb.

5. The community gossiper publicly tells a secret harmful to a neighbor's reputation, namely, that he was once a prisoner in a State prison. She claims that she has done this for the public good.

C. NUCLEAR WARFARE AND THE PRINCIPLE OF THE DOUBLE EFFECT. In our atomic age the concept of warfare has rapidly changed. Until the advent of nuclear weapons, bombing of enemy territory was on a more restricted scale. Such attacks could be morally justified as in the following case. A squadron of bombers attack an ammunition base vital to the enemy. It is foreknown from intelligence reports that some innocent civilians will be killed during the attack. Bombing itself is not a moral evil. The evil effect of killing some innocent civilians is not a means to the good effect of destroying the enemy's ammunition base. It is a by-product of the act of bombing the enemy base. The intention of the squadron of bombers is not to kill innocent civilians and there is a proportionately grave cause to allow such action: namely, the destruction of vital enemy ammunition.

Can the same be said of the case of a nuclear attack on a big city, for example, New York or Moscow? The type of bomb in question is a high megaton H bomb or one of similar destructive potentiality. Such bombs would destroy a large percentage of the population of a big city. There are of course atomic missiles of more restricted destructability.

President Eisenhower in an address given in February, 1957 on nuclear warfare commented: ". . . one bomb today can do the damage of probably all that we dropped on Germany in World War II. . . ." Thermonuclear explosions (H Bombs) are instruments of total warfare. In practice those responsible for such bombings cannot ordinarily avoid the direct intention of bombing the innocent civilian population. The physical destruction of these non-combatants cannot usually be taken as a by-product incidentally allied to a good effect. It is in essence part of what is effected. There is no proportionate reason to justify such wanton destruction of the innocent unless there would be an extraordinary military objective in the city itself. If the enemy has employed wanton bombing of cities, this does not make it right for the nation attacked to retaliate with like measures. There is no application of the principle of the twofold effect in thermonuclear bombing of cities ordinarily nor can it be justified by any other moral principle.

The manifest immorality of the Soviets is always a threat to the free nations. The United States is aware that if the Soviets have not yet actually threatened or employed such nuclear warfare, it is only because we are better or equally prepared for such warfare. The immorality of certain thermonuclear attacks on cities does not mean that the preparation of such bombs is itself immoral. There are instances where the uses of bombs of this kind seem to be licit, such as in an attack on an enemy fleet far out at sea or military targets sufficiently far away from areas of concentration of civilian population or even in a city having an extraordinary legitimate target: the leaders of the unjustly aggressive nation engaged in atomic warfare.

It is not yet certain nor probable that the effect of such explosions in the general environment is harmful to man. Meteorologists have found no evidence that atomic explosions have changed the weather or climate.[4] Radiation passes into the atmosphere and a great deal of it eventually returns to the ground as "fall out." Fall out is in three classes (1) close-in-material that comes down within a few hundred miles of the explosion and within 10 to 20 hours (2) intermediate-material that descends in a few weeks after the explosion (3) delayed-material that remains in the air for months or years.

Close-in-material would not affect cities in the cases given of bombing far out at sea or far away from areas inhabited by civilians. Intermediate fall out descends slowly and is mostly washed out by air, rain or snow. It can affect a small area, if there is a heavy precipitation while the radio-active cloud is overhead. Delayed fall out is stored for long periods in the atmosphere. Meteorologists know little about the duration of such material in the stratosphere and lower layers and where it may descend.

As regards atomic explosions in the deep parts of the ocean, materials deposited may remain there 100 years or more so that most of their radio-activity would be gone before they reach the surface water. However, what can be said of its effects on marine life? The report of the National Academy of Science reads:

> The committee has considered the question: "Has the atomic energy program as yet resulted in serious damage to marine life?" Its answer is "Probably no. . . . There is

[4] *The Biological Effects of Atomic Radiation* (Washington, D.C.: National Academy of Sciences—National Research Council, 1956), p. 5.

Confer also: A Commentary on the Report of the United Nations Scientific Committee on the Effects of Atomic Radiation (Washington, D.C.: National Academy of Sciences—National Research Council, 1959) 5 pages.

no evidence that any lasting damage has been done to the animal or plant population of the sea or large inland water bodies by the release of radioactive substances from weapons tests or reactors."[5]

However, an increase in atomic tests and large numbers of atomic plants dumping their deposits into the seas and inland waters would prove harmful. International control must be established in these matters for the good of mankind.

At present weapons tests are the chief source of artificial airborne radioactivity. In time, however, the atomic power industry will far outstrip military development in producing radioactive fission wastes. There is a moral obligation for human welfare that national and international controls be established for atomic power in its various uses in warfare and industry. If uncontrolled it can be a dangerous source of atmosphere radiation to plants, animals and man in present and future generations.[6] Radiation diseases that can afflict mankind are cancer and leukemia among others. Doses up to 100 roentgens when spread over years have been known to shorten human life. The evil effects cannot be treated as byproducts of the good effects to man in the case of contamination of the general atmosphere by the uncontrolled number of atomic warfare tests and the industrial plants. The cessation of atomic warfare tests by all nations would be a great safeguard to the good of our planet and its people.

Suggested Reading

Aristotle, *Nichomachean Ethics,* Bk. III, Chs. 1-5.

St. Thomas Aquinas, S. *Theol.,* P. I-II, q. 6.

M. Cronin, *The Science of Ethics* (Dublin: Gill & Son, 1930), Vol. 1, pp. 33-40.

F. J. Connell, C.SS.R., "Morality and the Atom Bomb," in *Thought Patterns* (Brooklyn: St. John's University, 1953), Vol. IV, pp. 55-67.

Questions

1. Define voluntariness, imputability, guilt.
2. Define and illustrate, actual intention, virtual intention.
3. a. What is a perfect voluntary act? Give a case of this kind of human act.

---

[5] *Ibid.,* p. 26.
[6] *The Biological Effects of Atomic Radiation, op. cit.,* p. 24.

b. What is an imperfect voluntary act? Give a case of this kind of human act.

4. Define a necessary and free voluntary act. Illustrate the necessary voluntary act.

5. When is a voluntary act positive and when is it negative?

6. Define and illustrate an act that is voluntary in itself and voluntary in cause.

7. What is the problem of the double effect?

8. State and explain the four principles that guide us in a case of the double effect.

9. Apply the principles of the double effect to high megaton H bomb warfare on a big city. State the instances where such bombing is licit and explain your reasons.

CHAPTER THREE

The Involuntary and Its Causes

I. DEFINITION AND DIVISION

THE STUDY of man seeking to fulfill his destiny is a study of human acts, the acts proper to man as a rational, free agent. There are many acts, however, that man performs in life which are not voluntary. They constitute acts for which he is not responsible and so do not move him toward his goal or away from it as a rational, free agent. Among the non-voluntary acts of man, there are involuntary acts which demand special study because they are sometimes completely involuntary and sometimes only in some respect involuntary.

The involuntary in man is a privation of the voluntary. The voluntary pertains to any act done from an intrinsic principle, the will, and with knowledge of the end. If an act is done by man without knowledge of the end or does not proceed from the intrinsic principle, the will, or lacks both of these elements, it is non voluntary. It simply lacks voluntariness. The involuntary is something more than this. The involuntary is an act which is contrary to one's will, committed either without knowledge of the end or without being willed or both. For example, a man passes on counterfeit money out of ignorance. This act is involuntary. It is contrary to his will to pass on counterfeits. He wills the passing on of what he believes is money but he does not will this end, namely, to pass on counterfeits.

The involuntary is divided into what is simply involuntary and what is involuntary in a certain respect. The simply involuntary is what one here and now does not will, for example, a person who is violently pushed aboard a train going to a destination other than his choice during a rush hour. The involuntary in a certain respect is what one *de facto* wills but which one would not will in other circumstances. A pilot orders his cargo thrown out because one of the motors of his trimotor plane is dead and he must maintain altitude. In ordinary circumstances the pilot would not order the cargo to be cast out. The action is involuntary in respect to ordinary circumstances but not in these circumstances of danger to plane and crew.

II. THE CAUSES OF INVOLUNTARY ACTS

General Ethics lists five causes that render an act involuntary so that a person is not judged to be responsible. They are ignorance, violence, fear, passion and habit. We shall treat each cause respectively as to its meaning, kinds, and effects in respect to destroying or lessening the voluntariness of an act.

A. IGNORANCE. 1. Meaning. "Ignorance causes involuntariness inasmuch as it deprives one of knowledge, which is a necessary condition of voluntariness..."[1] Ignorance signifies a lack of knowledge suitable to a person who should possess such knowledge. A student is called ignorant if he does not know the matter assigned to him in class. But he is certainly not ignorant if he does not know material given in the more advanced courses of the upper classes. Lack of knowledge is not the essence of ignorance but rather the lack of knowledge in a person who should have such knowledge. It should be noted that ignorance does not necessarily imply error, although it often actually is associated with error.

Sometimes a person does possess the knowledge suitable to him but here and now he does not recall it; this condition is called inadvertence. In such a case it cannot be said that a person is ignorant but rather that in this circumstance for some reason he does not advert to what he knows.

2. Division. By reason of influence on a person's action igno-

---

[1] *S. Theol.*, P. I-II, q. 6, a. 8.

rance is divided into antecedent, concomitant and consequent.[2] Antecedent ignorance is ignorance that occurs before an involuntary act and is the cause of it. For example, soldiers on a firing range take proper precaution to ascertain that no one is on the range before engaging in firing practice. A hunter disregarding the warning signs wanders on the range and is shot. Such ignorance on the part of the soldiers makes the act simply involuntary. The hunter's death was due to antecedent ignorance on the part of the soldiers.

Concomitant ignorance is ignorance of what is done but if it were known it would be done. If the hunter was an enemy of the soldier whose bullet killed him, and the soldier had the will to kill him, if he had the chance, the act done out of ignorance is non voluntary. However, it cannot be called involuntary because it is not contrary to the will of the agent.

Consequent ignorance is consequent to an act of the will insofar as the ignorance is itself voluntary. One wills to be ignorant and the consequent state of ignorance is due to the will either directly or indirectly. It is direct when a person affects ignorance. A person wishes to be ignorant of something that he can and should know as an excuse for his act. It is indirect when a person does not consider what he can and should know. He chooses to neglect to be informed out of some passion or habit.

Affected or direct consequent ignorance of a law both increases and decreases voluntariness. It increases voluntariness since the agent intends to use ignorance as an excuse for an act and it decreases voluntariness because the agent does not have the required knowledge to intend what is committed.[3] An example would be a person who affects ignorance on the morality of courtship as in the case of a young man who directly intends to avoid talks with his parents on moral conduct in dating. He directly intends ignorance in such matters because he deliberately wills to avoid being informed.

Indirect consequent ignorance is in a person who only indirectly wills the consequent ignorance. It is voluntary in cause inasmuch as one voluntarily neglects to be informed properly in some moral matter and the effect is at best only confusedly

2 S. *Theol.*, P. I-II, q. 6, a. 8.
3 Cajetan, *In* S. *Theol.*, 2-2, 150, 4, n. 5.

foreseen.[4] An example would be a youth who cannot find time to talk over the moral problems of dating with his parents because of his heavy social schedule. He keeps putting off talking with his parents not because he deliberately wills to affect ignorance in these moral matters but because he will not allow time for such talks. Although not as voluntary as affected or direct ignorance, such consequent ignorance is voluntarily caused by the agent.

By reason of the person who is ignorant, ignorance can be either vincible or invincible. Invincible ignorance is ignorance which is not in one's power to dispel. This is caused by the fact that one does not know that one lacks the required knowledge as in the case of some people who believe that artificial birth control is licit. They are victims of a pagan environment. Invincible ignorance can also be caused in a person who knows that he lacks the required knowledge but he cannot prudently overcome it. This is evidenced in a person who finds a lost article and cannot fine the owner.

Ignorance is vincible when it can be dispelled by prudent action. Whenever a state of ignorance is not dispelled due to one's own fault, it is vincible. A doctor who would fail to keep his medical knowledge up to date would be vincibly ignorant. A citizen who would fail to know the laws of the community in which he lives would be vincibly ignorant. By prudent action is meant that the effort employed to dispel the ignorance must be proportionate to the importance of the required knowledge. Ignorance in some light moral matter would not require the use of extraordinary means to dispel ignorance which is sometimes required in serious moral matters. Investigations to establish the freedom of a person to marry sometimes require years of inquiry in order to dispel ignorance and establish the certain fact that a person is here and now capable of entering into a true marriage.

Cases. I. Identify the following as a case of antecedent, concomitant or consequent ignorance. What can be said of the voluntariness or involuntariness of the act?

1. A man threatens his wife with a beating because she does not tend to her domestic duties. He sincerely means what

---

[4] P. Lombreros, *De Actibus Humanis* (Rome: Officium Libri Catholici, 1950), p. 31.

he says. Late that night believing that it is his daughter returning late, he slaps the woman several times, discovering that it is his wife.

2. The driver of a car stops at a busy crossroad and looks carefully before crossing. As he starts his car a pedestrian darts in front of the vehicle and is struck down. There was no opportunity for the driver to do otherwise.

3. A young lady is going steady with a serviceman with intentions to marry. She makes no effort to ascertain his freedom to marry other than his word that he was not married before. She knows very little about his background previous to their meeting at the military base. Although she knows that more inquiry is needed, she makes no effort to acquire the needed information.

4. A juror neglects to introduce a real doubt concerning the veracity of the principal witness in a murder trial because all the other jurors are convinced about the guilt of the accused. It is a hot day and they have been locked in for many hours. He prefers to remain in ignorance rather than to attempt to solve the doubt in a prolonged discussion and suffer the ire of his already fatigued fellow jurors.

II. Identify the following as invincible or vincible ignorance.

1. An airman is not sufficiently clear about the morality of a bombing mission that he is ordered to undertake. He could use his leave time to fly to another base where he could acquire the required knowledge from a chaplain. He decides that he should use his leave for a rest before this mission and attempts to forget the problem.

2. A student honestly claims that he cannot take the final examination because he has been too ill to study the required matter.

3. Voters neglect to investigate the capabilities of the candidates for election to public office because such inquiries would interfere with their business and pleasure.

4. While driving through Maryland, John was arrested for passing another car on a bridge. He claimed that this was his first time in Maryland and he did not know of such a law.

B. VIOLENCE. 1. Meaning. Violence is an exterior principle that forces the commission of an act contrary to the will of the passive subject.[5] A person who is physically forced to do something against his will is said to have acted under violence. One does not act according to one's own will and is physically forced to act according to the will of another. For example, a Hungarian patriot under torture is forced to admit that he has acted against the duly constituted People's Government of Hungary.

Violence does not reach the will directly. Its object is the external acts. Physical force cannot directly affect the will, a spiritual faculty. The body is the direct recipient of violence in some manner as by a beating. A person is free to will otherwise, no matter what the violence which impedes external acts. What is important is that the will of the recipient resists the evil will of the attacker. Whatever is done under violence is involuntary so long as the will resists it.

When the act one is forced to do is evil, one is always obliged to resist. There is no obligation, however, to use as much resistance as one can so long as one does not will the evil act that is being forced. A girl who is being forced to submit to an attacker against her virtue need not resist unto death. She may submit passively so long as her will opposes the deed and there is no proximate danger that she will consent to the resultant sensual pleasure. In such a case her participation is involuntary.

2. Division. Violence is either perfect or imperfect. It is perfect when the subject resists but cannot overcome the agent. Whatever is done under perfect violence is simply involuntary. If the victim resists less than he should, because he really intends the evil deed to occur, the violence is said to be imperfect. The person is not really being victimized by some agent compelling him to do what is against his will. The evil act is really voluntary, though it can be said to be partially involuntary. This would be the case if a man forced to steal resists only half heartedly, because he is not totally against joining in the theft.

Cases. Identify the following cases as acts of perfect or imperfect violence.

1. A woman is threatened with blackmail if she does not

---

[5] S. Theol., P. I-II, q. 6, a. 4, c.

pay a large sum of money to a person who knows a harmful secret of her past. She feels morally compelled to pay the money.

2. The Communist Secret Police prepare their victims for public confessions by brutalities which are sufficient to break down their physical resistance.

3. Some prisoners of war in Korea claimed they were forced to sign statements against the integrity of their country because they were given light beatings by their guards and knew that worse beatings would follow if they did not sign.

C. FEAR. 1. Meaning. Fear is the mental anxiety caused by an impending or future danger. It is a trepidation of the soul on account of some evil which is not present but which one believes will happen either very soon of in the near future.[6] It may be an emotional fear as a neurotic anxiety or an intellectual fear that arises from the studied knowledge of an evil that threatens one. Emotional fear is studied under passion as a cause of the involuntary. Our concern here is with intellectual fear. It must be noted that when we speak of intellectual fear we do not mean that fear has no emotional accompaniment but rather that it is a fear arising from some studied knowledge of a threat to one's security. It is opposed to a fear that is more rooted in one's emotions. Whereas violence is due to the force of action of an agent, an efficient cause, fear is in the order of a final cause, a motive that morally rather than physically can impel one to act due to the threat of an evil. It is in this sense that we speak of fear as a cause of the involuntary in man.

2. Division. On the part of the evil that threatens one, fear is either grave or light. If the danger that threatens one is of a proximate notable damage, the fear is grave, such as the fear of losing one's good name due to a recent threat. Fear is light if the damage threatened is notable but remote in respect to the present condition of a person, such as fear of suffering injury in a future war. Fear is also light if the damage that threatens is proximate but of light consequence, such as fear of any light penalty by a student who has broken a minor school regulation.

On the part of the influence which affects a person, fear

---

[6] S. *Theol.*, P. I-II, q. 6, a. 6.

may be antecedent or concomitant. It is antecedent when it precedes the act that it causes such as the fear that causes a man to hand over his wallet to an armed thief. It is concomitant when it occurs with an act but does not cause the act, as the fear of the thief that he will be caught in the act of robbery. Our concern is with antecedent fear as a cause of the involuntary in man.

Intellectual antecedent fear does not destroy the voluntariness of an act as St. Thomas says: "... that which is done out of fear is essentially voluntary because its principle is from within ..."[7] St. Thomas further explains: "In what is done from compulsion, the will does nothing inwardly; whereas in what is done through fear, the will does something."[8]

Emotional fear such as great anxiety can cause an act to be involuntary. Intellectual fear takes place in one who knows that an evil can happen to him and makes a deliberate choice to avoid it. One could choose to accept the evil and its consequences but one chooses to avoid it. Antecedent intellectual fear lessens the voluntariness of the act because one would not will it in different circumstances. For example, a person would not pay a blackmailer unless there was present a fear that he would otherwise reveal a shameful secret of one's past. Such actions are only in some respect involuntary; they are not simply involuntary. Only when the accompanying emotional fear is so strong as to blind reason and put one in a state of emotional unbalance can it be said that acts done out of fear are simply involuntary. But this is not the case with intellectual fear as such.

Antecedent, intellectual, grave fear does not excuse one from acts that are intrinsically evil such as to lie, steal or indulge in illicit sexual practices. It does excuse one from observing the positive law because where the common good is not endangered, a legislator cannot oblige with a grave inconvenience. This is the case with contracts drawn up out of grave fear that is unjustly inspired from without; marriages or vows contracted in this condition are not binding.

Cases. Are the following actions done out of antecedent intel-

---

[7] S. *Theol.*, P. I-II, q. 6, a. 6.
[8] S. *Theol.*, P. I-II, q. 6, a. 6, ad 1.

lectual fear? Are they voluntary, involuntary simply or involuntary in some respect?

1. A union official invokes the fifth amendment by which privilege he is excused from giving evidence against himself. He takes the fifth amendment out of fear of involving himself in a long prison term which would be certain for him if he gave the evidence desired by the cross-examining counsel.

2. Untrained Chinese soldiers in the Korean war often abandoned their positions in fright during a direct bayonet attack by U.N. troops.

3. Joan claims that she did not really contract a valid marriage with Paul because at the time of the ceremony she feared that he would not want children and subsequent events proved her correct.

4. Out of fear of causing a scene and losing her position, the secretary submits to improper advances from her employer.

5. Before the marriage Cornelia's mother threatens to kill herself unless she goes through with the marriage with the Count. It seems certain that her mother means what she threatens.

6. A counter-intelligence agent captured by the Chinese Communists out of fear of revealing vital information to the enemy under torture takes a suicide pill.

D. PASSION. 1. Meaning. Passion is a movement in the sense appetite caused by the imaginative awareness of the presence of good or evil and productive of some change in the body.[9] It is not a movement of the intellect or the will but rather in the sense appetite caused by some vivid realization in the imagination of the presence of good or evil. It produces some bodily change as anger causes the face to flush, the heart to beat rapidly and so forth. It should be noted that passion is not restricted to the sexual appetite.

Passions are neither good nor evil morally considered. They are natural to the rational animal. What renders them good or evil is their deliberate use toward what is good or evil by the rational will. Anger, fear, love, hate and so forth can be good if their objects, motives and circumstances are commensurate with the person concerned.

---

[9] S. Theol., P. I-II, q. 6, a. 7.

Aristotle divided the passions into the concupiscible and the irascible. The concupiscible pertain to goods that are easily obtainable, and the irascible to goods that are difficult to obtain.

CONCUPISCIBLE PASSIONS — TOWARD OBJECTS EASILY OBTAINED

In Respect to the Good	*In Respect to Evil*
Love	Hate
Desire	Aversion
Joy	Sorrow

IRASCIBLE PASSIONS — TOWARD OBJECTS DIFFICULT TO OBTAIN

In Respect to the Good	*In Respect to Evil*
Hope	Courage
Despair	Fear

This division is not exclusive. It is presented simply to illustrate certain kinds of passion. In popular context passion is very often taken to signify anger or love. The signification is far more extensive. The psychological analysis of passion is not our aim in this study. Our concern is the way passion affects the voluntariness of an act.

2. Division of Passion in Respect to the Voluntary. Passions may be antecedent or consequent to the action of the will. Antecedent passion arises spontaneously from bodily states independent of the will. Sometimes when an object is presented to the senses there is an automatic response, a sudden bodily reaction occurs as of desire or aversion. They occur in us without our will. Antecedent passion of this kind is an act of man but not a human act.

Consequent passion is consequent on the action of the will which excites the passions in some way. For example, brooding over some misfortune can arouse us to anger. Consequent passion is a human act. Deliberate attendance at indecent movies, deliberate reading of lascivious literature, deliberate taking part in smutty stories inasmuch as they produce an excitation of the sexual appetite, deliberately bring about consequent passions.

Antecedent passion can bring about simply involuntary acts. When the passion is so strong as to prevent the use of reason, the act done under its influence is not a human act. This could be the case in a passion of violent anger or extreme fear. Usually, however, antecedent passion does not destroy freedom, but it diminishes the voluntariness of acts done under its influence. It can render what is objectively a grave offense a light offense by reason of lessening the imputability of the act. Illicit carnal thoughts can arise from bodily dispositions and be present in the imagination without consent or with a semi-deliberate adherence which lessens their imputability. Acts done in a passion are always less free than acts done with premeditation and without disturbing bodily influences.

Consequent passion does not lessen the voluntariness of an act but it can increase it. Passions that are deliberately aroused are voluntary in themselves. A person who deliberately puts himself in a proximate occasion of sin, knows that his passions will be aroused. The excitation of the passions is directly willed. What results from the passion is either voluntary in itself or in cause. If a person arouses his passions as a means for some evil end then the consequent evil is voluntary in itself. The fact that one deliberately acts to strengthen one's tendency to evil increases the voluntariness of his act, such as a man who gets himself slightly intoxicated to enkindle his anger. If a person knows beforehand that he will be induced to a certain act by his passions, even though the act is not willed in itself, as it is affected by the influence of the deliberate passion and foreseen as an effect it is indirectly voluntary. A person who deliberately becomes angered foreseeing that his anger will cause him to blaspheme, indirectly wills the blasphemy even though he lost control of himself in the anger causing the blasphemy. The blasphemy is voluntary in cause because he willed the anger which he knew would cause it.

Cases. Identify the following cases of antecedent or consequent passion. If it is voluntary specify whether the voluntariness is increased or decreased.

1. In the barracks a group of soldiers pass around indecent pictures. A young inductee is troubled in conscience by the fact that he was shown the pictures, although he had no will to share in this indecent pastime.

2. Fear of sex has been identified with modesty in Joan's imagination. She fears to be alone with her escort, although she knows that he is a virtuous young man.

3. A young couple in courtship frequently spend many hours alone in his apartment. They frequently fall into carnal sins. They contend that they cannot help themselves because of their love for one another.

4. An employee dwells constantly on the insults he has received from his employer. He arouses his anger so that he curses his employer and develops a hatred for him.

E. HABIT. Habit is a constant way of acting caused by repeated acts. Morally speaking habits are good or evil. As virtue is a habit of doing good, vice is a habit of doing evil. Once a habit is formed acts follow from it spontaneously so that deliberate guidance is either unnecessary or lessened. Childhood and youth are important in the formation of good moral habits of acting.

A habit is voluntary in itself when it is being learned. Once learned it can become so automatic that it is either only voluntary in cause or it lessens voluntariness because there is little advertence to the act itself. A person who has matured in good moral habits usually has a greater facility in performing good acts. Many adults who are troubled by marital problems or difficulties in getting along with people socially, and who are even a menace to the public good, are the product of a childhood illformed by neglectful parents, and a progressive education which stressed personal liberty rather than responsibilities to God and one's fellow man. They have acquired habits of thought and action which are rooted in exaggerated selfishness.

If one does not deliberately acquire a habit, one is not responsible for it in cause, although one has the responsibility to remove it if it is evil. Usually in the moral life one deliberately acquires habits; at least there is some advertence. Once one realizes that an evil habit is being formed one is bound to correct it. If nothing is done to remove it, the habit is voluntary at least in cause. When a person is a victim of some habit as swearing or excessive drinking, such acts will be spontaneous so long as one does not remove the cause of the habit continuing. A man who knows that he will drink too much so long as he follows a certain recreational pattern, for example, to frequent a bar where his cronies drink until they are fully inebriated, such a person is responsible for putting himself into an occasion of an evil habit.

The effort that we use to correct a bad habit must be proportionate to the gravity of the evil done. Far more effort is required for removing a habit of drug addiction or alcoholism than for the habit of telling small lies. Addiction to any habit is conditioned by circumstances, which must be rearranged to insure a safe cure. Effort must be made not only in respect to external circumstances but also to the correction of the internal circumstances of motivation. Self analysis, the uprooting of egotism, which is at the root of every bad habit, the ability to admit that one is wrong and to take the steps toward correction, such things take almost heroic effort on the part of the person habituated to a gravely evil habit. Sometimes a pyschiatrist's aid is required as well as special moral guidance toward effecting the correction of an evil habit.

Special attention must be given to the increasing evil habit of alcoholism. It was estimated in 1952 by the United States Public Health Service that there are four million alcoholics in our nation. All of these people are not on skid row. Some come from good families and from respectable sections of town and country. They are for the most part people who began to drink with no intention of overdoing what is in itself a legitimate recreational practice. At the start of their social drinking they were masters of their drinking but in time the drink mastered them. The social drinker is in control of the drink and of himself; the drunkard is in control of neither. Very often the drunkard is suffering from some mental ill, which causes excessive drinking. He is always an emotionally immature person, who refuses to face reality and attempts to detour from responsibility by over-indulging in drinking. Chronic alcoholism cannot in all cases be dismissed as simply involuntary or compulsive.

Cases. Identify the following cases of habitual evils as voluntary or involuntary. If the case involves voluntary action, is this voluntary in itself or in cause?

1. In many juvenile parties petting has become customary so that one can say that these teenagers are habituated to illicit intimacies. Criticize the opinion of some psychoanalysts that such actions are compulsory habits as natural consequences of our anxious age.

2. A chronic alcoholic on skid row craves more drink in a

state of alcoholic hallucination in which he hears voices telling him to procure more "canned heat."

3. The sergeant has a habit of swearing. He invariably employs certain blasphemous and carnal vocabulary when he becomes angered.

4. John has a habit of lying when he is caught doing wrong. He has cultivated a habit of irresponsibility which causes him to shift the blame to others.

Suggested Reading

Aristotle, *Nicomachean Ethics,* Bk. III, chs. 1-5.
St. Thomas Aquinas, *S. Theol.,* P. I II, q. 6, as 4-8.
W. Farrell, *Companion to the Summa,* Vol. II, chs. v, vi, vii, x.
J. Cavanagh and J. McGoldrick, *Fundamental Psychiatry* (Milwaukee; Bruce, 1953).

Questions

1. What is meant by the involuntary? Does it connote the same meaning as the non-voluntary?
2. Define the simply involuntary and the involuntary in a certain respect. Illustrate your reply.
3. State the five causes of involuntary acts. Define each.
4. What is meant by antecedent, concomitant, and consequent ignorance. Illustrate and discuss the voluntariness or involuntariness of each.
5. What is meant by direct and indirect consequent ignorance? Illustrate each. What can be said of their voluntariness and involuntariness?
6. Define and illustrate vincible and invincible ignorance. Discuss their voluntariness or involuntariness.
7. When is violence said to be perfect? Imperfect? Are these acts voluntary or involuntary?
8. Distinguish emotional and intellectual fear.
9. When is fear said to be grave? Light?
10. Define and illustrate antecedent and concomitant fear.
11. What kind of fear are we concerned with in this analysis of fear as a cause of the involuntary? Discuss its voluntariness and involuntariness.
12. What are concupiscible passions? Irascible passions? Illustrate each.
13. Define antecedent and consequent passion. Illustrate each. What can be said of their voluntariness and involuntariness?
14. Define habit. Discuss the voluntariness and involuntariness of habits.

CHAPTER FOUR

The Morality of Human Acts

I. INTRODUCTION: THE PROBLEM OF MORALITY

WHAT IS THE REASON for judging that some human acts are good and others are evil? Do we make moral judgments because the moral order is founded in the very nature of things or are our moral judgments the result of habits of education, environment, heredity? Is the moral law universally the same for all men or is it a variable that varies from age to age and from place to place? Can one logically speak of such a thing as the moral law or should one rather refer to moral sentiments, moral viewpoints?

This is basically a philosophical problem which more or less confronts all of us at some time in our lives. It may be reduced simply to the question: May a person pick and choose morals or is there a moral law made by a Supreme Authority for man and given to his rational nature? In some manner or other this question arises in moral discussions either in speculation or in practice. One must either assume that morals are made by man or made for man by a higher authority. If morality is man-made then morals must be relative, arbitrary, subjective. If morals are given in the very nature of our species by God Who has authority over the very nature of things, then morals must be objective, universal and necessary.

The answer that one makes to this problem of morality may determine one's judgment in the whole gamut of moral issues on rights and duties, sanction and obligation, virtues and vices. It has the power to give direction and meaning to one's judgments on particular moral questions such as atomic control, euthanasia, abortion, artificial birth control, capital and labor, courtship, marriage, duties to God in the virtue of religion.

The Thomistic analysis of the destiny of man realized in God, Who is man's ultimate end, the meaning of human acts as the natural means toward man's Supreme End, and the study of the voluntary and involuntary in man are important antecedents to the study of the moral life of man. Morality can only have meaning for us philosophically after we understand the questions: What is God? What is man? What is the purpose of human life and what is the meaning of human acts? Radically the meaning of morality is drawn out of knowing God and myself. There is a priority here in the order of nature. Erroneous concepts of God and man must produce erroneous notions of morality.

The objective, metaphysical analysis of morality must first of all consider the nature of our acts and then the accidents or circumstances as these contribute to the rightness or wrongness of things. This is the moralist's analysis of the object or nature of a human act and its circumstances and motive or the accidents.

II. THE DETERMINANTS OF MORALITY: THE OBJECT, END AND CIRCUMSTANCES OF THE HUMAN ACT

The determinants whereby we judge a human act to be good or evil are found in the object, end and circumstances of the human act. Let us consider each of these respectively.

A. THE OBJECT: The object of a human act is the first specifying determinant. The good or evil of anything is determined by its perfection or fullness of being as was seen. The primary element in the perfection of a thing is its form which gives it species. This is what is meant by the object of a human act: it is the very form of the human act, its essential meaning as a specific kind of human act such as the human act of telling the truth or its contrary, of lying, of practicing justice or its contrary, stealing, and so forth. The object specifies the human act.[1] It must be noted that object in this context does not mean the goal or end of the human act but rather its form.

If an object by its nature is suitably proportioned to the rational nature as related to the ultimate end, the object is morally good. The human acts of love of God, of temperance, of justice are called good for this reason. On the other hand, the human acts that are not proportionate to the rational nature as related to its ultimate end are always morally evil such as to lie, to steal, to murder.

The identification of the moral species of an action is important. This is done at length in moral theology. It suffices in *General Ethics* that the student be acquainted with the natural foundations for such specification. The species of lying is a voluntary utterance contrary to intellectual conviction. Lying is not specified by the fact that one tells an untruth because one may not be mentally aware that a thing is untrue. Theft is the secret removal of another's goods against the owner's reasonable will. Theft is not simply the secret removal of something that belongs to another. It must be against the reasonable will of another. For example, a person who is starving may secretly take food that belongs to one who has plenty, if this is the only way that he can sustain himself. There was nothing illicit done when Father Kapaun secretly removed food from his Chinese captors to feed his fellow American prisoners of war. This cannot be specified as theft. It is agreed by all moralists that in extreme need a person may take so much of the goods of another as will free him from his present necessity.

The object of murder is the direct and unjust killing of another human being. Murder is not specified by taking the life of another; rather it must be directly willed and it must be done without legitimate authority. The soldier who kills in battle, the state executioner who puts criminals to death, cannot be specified as murderers. So too one who kills in reasonable self defense is not a murderer because this is authorized by the natural law.

B. THE CIRCUMSTANCES OF A HUMAN ACT: Morality is not only determined by the object or the form of a human act; circumstances also affect human acts making them morally good or evil.

---

[1] *S. Theol.*, P. I-II, q. 18, prologue.

The circumstances are the accidentals or conditions that adhere to the human act itself such as: when did it happen, where did it happen, by what means did it happen, who did it, to whom was it done, how often was it committed, and so forth. Circumstances can aggregate or lessen the goodness or evil of a human act. For example, lying is always evil but to lie in matters that gravely affect our neighbor's character is more evil than to lie in light matters as in breaking a merely social engagement. Stealing is always wrong but to steal from a wealthy man the amount of a laborer's day's wages is not the grave evil of stealing that amount from a laborer.

Circumstances sometimes add a distinct specification to an act apart from its object. For example, unchastity is any misuse of the sexual faculties but if at least one of the parties is married to another the evil is adultery.

C. THE END: The end is really the circumstance of deliberate motive: why an act is done. This is what the ethician means by end as a determinant of morality. For example, in gossiping the end may be to ruin another's good reputation. One may have a good motive for performing an evil object such as to steal in order to donate to charity. But a human act is vitiated by its defects and so the act is objectively evil. It is possible, however, for a person to be so attentive to the good end that the evil of an act may escape him as in the case of a person so given to telling the truth that he may reveal the faults of another to persons who have no right to such knowledge. Such acts although inculpable are objectively morally wrong.

When the end and object are both good or both evil we distinguish two possibilities. Firstly if the object is by its very nature related to the end there is only one kind of goodness or evil present as when one is chaste in body in order to be pure of heart before God or if one steals in order to enrich oneself wrongfully. If, however, the object is not by its very nature related to the end but is ordered to the end by the deliberate designs of the agent, there is more than one kind of moral goodness or evil in the act. This is the case when one lies in order to commit a theft. The morality of the act is determined not simply as a lie but a lie in order to steal. Lying of itself is not related to stealing but it is rendered so by the intention of the agent. St. Thomas explains that an act can have more than one moral species.

> ... an action which as to its substance is in one natural species, considered in respect to the moral conditions that are added to it, can belong to two species.[2]

III. THE NUMERICAL DISTINCTION OF MORAL ACTS

Moral acts are distinguished not only in species or kind of good or evil but also in number. It should be noted that one and the same act of the will accompanied by one external act can have more than one moral evil in number. A man who intends to kill twenty men in one explosion, when this is done, commits twenty murders. The species of the moral evil is murder and the number of murders is twenty. A person who intends to seduce two people by telling one smutty story commits two sins. However, a man who intends to seduce a woman and immediately before or after indulges in immodest speech, looks or caresses commits acts that are of one moral object: namely the evil of lust.

There are as many evils as there are moral interruptions of the will. In purely internal moral evils such as carnal thoughts, these are interrupted by physical cessations such as performing some work. Unless the interval is very brief another moral evil in number takes place if one returns to such thoughts afterwards. Acts that are partly internal and partly external such as theft are not broken by physical cessations, as in the case of a man who intends to steal $100 from his employer in small amounts in a month's time. This is one act of theft. External acts are not interrupted by any involuntary cessation, provided that the cessation is not for a long time and the acts have morally complete objects. This happens in the case of a burglar who is interrupted in his act by a policeman passing by and who continues when the policeman has gone. This is one moral act of theft. There are as many different moral evils in number (in the same species) as there are distinct acts of the will and total objects of the acts.

[2] S. Theol., P. I-II, q. 18, a. 7, ad 1.

IV. THESIS: HUMAN ACTS ARE GOOD OR EVIL AS THEY CONFORM OR DO NOT CONFORM TO THE RULE OF MORALS

A. SENSE OF THE THESIS: The thesis means that every human act is either good or evil according to an objective moral standard. Although there are indifferent acts in the abstract, there are no indifferent acts in the concrete. A human act must be either good or evil and it is so by an objective moral standard. For example, drinking alcoholic beverages is indifferent as such, that is, in the abstract. In a concrete situation as a human act, an act done with deliberate intention, it is either good or evil morally considered.

B. DEFINITION OF TERMS: By a human act is meant an act that proceeds from the will with knowledge of the end.

Good means that a thing has its due perfection. A good human act has the perfection due to it morally: the human act is in accord with a rational nature in following its end. Evil is the lack of perfection due to a thing. "Evil results from a single defect, whereas good results from a complete cause."[3] Moral evil is a disproportion of a human act to its rational nature in seeking its end. The rule of morals refers to the standard whereby man judges a human act as good or evil. This standard is determined by the object, circumstances and the end of the human act. It is sometimes called the constituent norm of morality because it is the standard for determining what is right and what is wrong and also the species of the human act as right or wrong, i.e., an act of heroic charity, an act of murder. It is manifested to man by right reason.

The standard of morality can be ultimate or proximate. Ultimately it is God, the Author of the good. Proximately it is human nature. In this thesis we are concerned with the proximate, constitutive norm of morality.

C. ERRORS: All who are relativists: Those who contend that morals are not determined by a universal standard but that morals are dependent on something subjective. Immanuel Kant (1724-1804), who denied that man can objectively know causes and essences, supplied what he called the categorical imperatives

---

[3] *S. Theol.*, P. I-II, q. 18, a. 4, ad 3.

as a rule of morals: These may be summed up in the axiom: So act that your maxim may become a universal law.[4] Lying must be wrong not because it is wrong by its very nature according to Kant but rather because one could not make lying a rule of action for all men.

English moralists of the seventeenth and eighteenth century founded morality in man's sentiments. Anthony Shaftesbury (1671-1713) stated that it is man's sense of right and wrong that determines morality. "Sense of right and wrong, therefore, being as natural to us as natural affection . . . there is no speculative opinion, persuasion or belief, which is capable immediately or directly to exclude or destroy it."[5]

Thomas Reid (1710-1796) of the Scottish School affirmed morality to be "an original faculty in man whereby we perceive certain things to be right, others to be wrong."[6] Adam Smith (1723-1790) wrote a *Theory of Moral Sentiments* in which he held that morals depend on man's sentiment of propriety.[7]

Another extreme trend attempts to find the origin of morals in the society in which one lives. Thomas Hobbes (1588-1679), perhaps influenced by the moral upheavals of the English Revolution, believed that right and wrong is determined by the law.[8] According to Auguste Comte (1798-1857) morality is recorded in the fact of human life, the way in which people conduct themselves.[9] In our own time John Dewey taught: "Customs constitute moral standards."[10] Oliver Wendell Holmes, the famed American jurist, wrote: ". . . our system of morals is a body of imperfect social generalizations expressed in terms of emotion."[11]

---

[4] I. Kant, *Critique of Practical Reason*, transl. by Abbott. (London, New York: Longmans, Green, 1927).

[5] A. Shaftesbury, *Characteristics of Men, Manner, Opinions, Times.* Vol. II, p. 22.

[6] T. Reid, *Essays on the Active Powers of the Human Mind.* (Edinburgh: Bell, 1788), p. 236.

[7] A. Smith, *The Theory of Moral Sentiments* (London: Bell, 1880), pp. 479, 480.

[8] T. Hobbes, Leviathan (Molesworth), Vol. III, p. 115.

[9] L. Levy-Bruhl, *The Philosophy of Auguste Comte,* trans. by F. Harrison (New York: Putnam, 1903), p. 307.

[10] J. Dewey, *Human Nature and Conduct* (New York: Holt, 1922), p. 75.

[11] O. W. Holmes, *Collected Legal Papers* (New York: Harcourt Brace, 1920), p. 306.

Morals for Holmes are prejudices, tastes due to one's environment.[12]

In the trend of Auguste Comte and Emile Durkeim ethics has become in many centers of learning a branch of sociology. *The Encyclopedia of the Social Sciences* describes morals as:

> ... the sum of taboos and prescriptions in the folk-ways by which right conduct is defined. Right conduct is what the group approves of, wrong conduct what the group disapproves of.[13]

The Communist judgment of human conduct given by the Soviet Dictator, Nikolai Lenin judges morality as determined by the class struggle. Whatever benefits Communism is good, all else is evil.

> We repudiate all morality taken apart from human society and classes. We say that it is deception, a fraud, a befogging of the minds of the workers and peasants by the landlords and capitalists.[14]

Contact of Americans with Japanese culture has given rise to the current fad called "Zen." This form of Buddhist pantheism regards the world as illusory and holds there is no real difference between good and evil.

D. Proof of the Thesis. The good is that which conforms to the nature of a being and evil is what does not conform to a being's nature.

But the rule of morality is nothing else than the order of agreement or disagreement of human acts to human nature.

Therefore, human acts are good or evil as they conform or do not conform to the rule of morality.

Proof of the Major. This is evident from what has been said in Part One concerning the meaning of good and evil. St. Thomas says:

> Good and evil are of constitutive difference only in morals, which receives its species from the end, which is the object of the will, on which morals depend. And because good has the reason of the end, therefore, good and

---

[12] *Holmes-Pollock Letters,* ed. M. O. Howe (Cambridge, Mass., Harvard Press, 1941), Vol. I, p. 105.
[13] "Morals," Vol. X, p. 643.
[14] Nikolai Lenin: *Selected Works* (Moscow: Foreign Language Publishing House, 1951), Vol. II, part 2, p. 482.

evil are specific differences in morals: good *per se* but evil, inasmuch as it is the remotion of an owed end.[15]

Proof of the Minor. Morality is the standard whereby we judge what is good and what is evil. Although it is revealed to man by reason, it is not merely a relation of reason but rather a transcendental relation found in our human nature. Right reason as the faculty of being judges what is right because it knows that the human act is proportionate to our human nature ordered to an end, evil is disproportionate. For example, to tell the truth is good because our speech concurs with what our mind knows to be true; to lie is to lack this perfection which is proper to man.

E. FALSE STANDARDS OF MORALITY: In the other systems of morality cited, morality is not a standard that is universal and true corresponding objectively to the human being in pursuit of its proper ends. These systems lack a true metaphysics; they fail to establish morality on the real and found it on the subjective.

Kant's categorical imperative is probably the most outstanding example of a subjective norm of morality. According to Kant man cannot know any nature or essence but only appearances or phenomena. On the phenomenal level one knows what is right and wrong because some things are practically right and some things are practically wrong. This is the categorical imperative: Act as if your maxim can be a universal law. This principle, however, fails by defect because it supposes all moral goods are preceptive or matters of duty. There are many moral goods that are matters of counsel such as acts of charity, which although morally good cannot be commanded of all as a universal law. Furthermore, what is preceptive is good essentially not because it can be universally practiced but because it conforms to human nature which is shared by all. How can one know what is universally good in practice unless one knows that something conforms to the human nature, the universal subject of contingent moral practices.

Feelings or sentiments cannot be the common standard of the moral good and evil for man because they are variable both from person to person and from time to time in the life of a person. Furthermore, feelings terminate in the sensible

---

[15] *In 8 Metaph.*, lect. 2, n. 1694.

good; morals in the perfective good, as was shown in Part One. What may be pleasant for the senses may not be perfective of a human person. A person may have good feelings or sentiments and at the same time have bad morals.

Morality cannot be an innate faculty in man whereby all men perceive what is right and wrong, precisely because although morality is universal as a standard, it is not *de facto* universally found the same as known by all men due to defects in education, environment and so forth. Reason is impaired by these factors and they cannot be reconciled with any common inborn faculty of moral perception as Reid defines it.

Morality is not a standard by custom essentially, although morals as practiced by men can become customary to a people. Some morals are determined by man-made laws, for example, traffic laws. But morality is not essentially a legal standard devised by man. It is a standard founded in human nature essentially and if man makes laws in addition to what is natural, it is to supplement or to enunciate more clearly what is natural. The penal laws pertaining to homicide exist only because it is naturally evil to murder.

Finally morals are not essentially taboos or prejudices defended by emotions, although they can falsely become such in people. There is a difference between the moral standard manifested by right reason and how some people practice "morality." In America morals for some people is in part a system of taboos and prejudices against smoking, any use of alcoholic beverages, dancing, all games of chance. Antagonists to this extreme trend sometimes oppose morals as if constituted essentially of these conventional biases of some communities.

Suggested Reading

Aristotle, *Nicomachean Ethics,* Bk. IX, ch. 8.
St. Thomas Aquinas, S. *Theol.,* I-II, qs. 7, 18, 19, 20, *Contra Gent.* Bk. III, ch. 129.
Henri Renard, "The Existential Moral Act," in *The New Scholasticism,* Vol. XXVIII (1954), pp. 145-169.

Questions

1. Discuss what is meant by the problem of morality.
2. Define and illustrate the determinants of morality: the object, circumstances and end of the human act.

3. What is meant by the principle: the circumstances can change the morality of an act?

4. How can an act although physically one in kind be twofold or many in its moral species? Illustrate.

5. How are moral acts numerically distinguished?

6. State the thesis on the morality of human acts.
   a. Define the terms.
   b. Cite some modern errors against the thesis.
   c. Prove the thesis.

7. Demonstrate that morality is not the same as duty (Kant's categorical imperative), animate faculty, sentiment, custom, the law of a state.

CHAPTER FIVE

The Virtues

I. THE MEANING OF MORAL VIRTUE

A PERSON IS SAID to lead a virtuous life when he habitually conforms his life to the moral standard. A person is not said to be virtuous because he has been known in some instances to tell the truth or because there is very little larceny in his life or because he is sober most of the week. *Virtue is a habit of doing good.* It is acquired by repeated acts of doing good.

Virtue in general can be physical or intellectual or moral. It is the excellence of a thing according to its due perfection. It is the virtue of the eye to see, the intellect to know. A vice is a lack of due perfection in a thing.
Aristotle explains:

> Every virtue both brings into good condition the thing of which it is the excellence and makes the work of that thing to be well done ... therefore the virtue of a man will be a state of character which makes a man good and makes him do his own work well.[1]

St. Augustine defines moral virtue as "a good quality of the mind by which one lives righteously, of which no one can make bad use ..."[2] Virtue is called "a quality" because it is an operative habit, an ordered disposition of the soul, difficult

---

[1] Aristotle, *Nichomachean Ethics*, Bk. II, 6, 1106a.
[2] St. Augustine, *On Free Will*, II, 19.

to remove and acquired by repeated acts. It is a habit affecting one's powers of action. Virtue is said to be a "quality of the mind" since moral virtue is a certain participation of reason in the acts of the will and the total goodness of moral virtue depends on the rectitude of reason. This does not mean that a man is said to be a man of virtue because he has good judgments of the moral life. The intellect is said to be the subject of moral virtue insofar as it is subordinate to the will. "If man does well actually, this is because he has a good will."[3] It is a "good quality" because it perfects a person in some way, "by which one lives righteously," that is according to the moral standard. "Of which no one can make bad use" means that moral virtue is always good as opposed to something that is sometimes good and sometimes evil.

II. THE KINDS OF VIRTUES

Virtue as an operative habit can affect any power of the soul. There are physical virtues that affect the corporeal powers such as health and beauty. There are intellectual virtues that affect the intellect, wisdom, science and understanding. Wisdom considers the highest causes. Science considers the proper causes of things. There are many sciences but only one wisdom. Understanding is the knowledge of self-evident first principles. These virtues perfect the speculative intellect. Art, the right reason of things to be made, perfects the practical intellect. Prudence also perfects the practical intellect as the right reason of things to be done. The moral virtues perfect the will in ordering human acts to their proper ends.

Speculative intellectual virtue is not the same as moral virtue. Only prudence is an intellectual virtue and also a moral virtue.[4] A person is not morally virtuous because he knows well the science of ethics. It is only when a person's will, enlightened by moral principles by the intellect, habitually does good, that moral virtue is present. Inasmuch as intellect and will are really distinct faculties of the soul, the virtues proper to these faculties are said to be specifically distinct. One may possess

---

[3] S. Theol., P. I-II, q. 56, a. 3.
[4] Ibid., P. I-II, q. 58, a. 2 and 3.

the speculative intellectual virtue of the science of ethics and be without moral virtue.

Socrates on the contrary, according to Xenophon, taught knowledge is virtue:

> Those who knew what were just and righteous acts would prefer nothing else, while those who would not know them could not do them if they would.[5]

The whole subject of the dialogue "Meno" is Plato's teaching that moral virtue is intellectual virtue. Whereas it is true that moral virtue presupposes right judgment, it cannot be said that right judgment necessitates moral living. Experience as well as reason shows the contrary. There are some educators and social thinkers in our times who seem to advocate this Socratic error: that knowledge is moral virtue. It is evidenced in the belief that education formally produces good moral citizens, that courses in sex hygiene dispel promiscuity, that good schools are the primary agency against juvenile delinquency. The moral discipline of a good home in which the parental love and authority guide the young in the formation of the moral virtues is sadly neglected in many instances.

Furthermore, moral virtue is not the same as the practical intellectual virtue of art. A person adept in the arts is not thereby made a morally good person. The object of the arts is producing something as in the fine arts or in the mechanical arts. Art, St. Thomas says, is "the right reason of things to be made."[6] The moral virtue of prudence, however, concerns "the right reason of things to be done."[7] It is not merely an intellectual virtue because it rectifies the will in acting to an end and so it is also a moral virtue. Art in some way concerns a production in the material order except the liberal arts which concern production in the intellectual order as in making good arguments. The liberal arts are in the speculative order. Prudence concerns doing, the ordering of human acts whereby man is disposed properly toward his ends in the moral life. Rectitude of the will is essential to prudence but not to art

---

[5] Xenophon, *Memorabilia*, III, c. IX, 5.
[6] *S. Theol.*, P. I-II, q. 57, a. 4.
[7] *Ibid.*, q. 61, a. 1.

which pertains to the perfection of the work done. St. Thomas explains:

> Right reason which is in accord with prudence is included in the definition of moral virtue, not as a part of its essence, but as something belonging by way of participation to all the moral virtues, insofar as they are all under the direction of prudence.[8]

Sometimes the man of artful industry, the person who has an aptness for good work, is regarded as the man of moral virtue. Very often this sort of person is regarded as the ideal in the technological society. He is the prudent man. In America the shape of many peoples' destiny is chartered by the economic character of our society. The big corporation has certain ideals whereby a person must live in service to the company as a kind of vital standard. The right of a company to impose certain ideals of practical intellectual virtue for the sake of efficiency is of course expected. However, the identification of the art of technical skills or of business efficiency with the moral virtues, as if such skills and efficiency are the virtues that determine the moral goodness of a person, is without foundation in reality. A person may be industrious, thrifty, skilled in his art of producing and at the same time be immoral. Success in material production does not always mean moral achievement as a human person. The artful man need not be the prudent man.

Moral virtue can be without the intellectual virtues of wisdom, science and art but not without the intellectual virtues of understanding and prudence.[9] Prudence is an intellectual and also a moral virtue. Prudence which is the right reason of things to be done is necessary to the moral life because a good life consists in good deeds and in order to do good deeds it matters not only what a man does but how he does it.[10] A man is suitably directed to his end by prudence, an intellectual virtue which perfects the reason and makes it suitably affected toward things ordained to the end. The intellectual virtue of understanding is necessary to the moral life because it pertains to the knowledge of self-evident principles such as "do good and

---

[8] *S. Theol.*, P. I-II, q. 58, a. 2, ad 4.
[9] *Ibid.*, q. 58, a. 4.
[10] *Ibid.*, q. 57, a. 5.

avoid evil." The intellectual and moral virtue of prudence pre-supposes understanding of the self-evident principles.

III. THE CARDINAL VIRTUES

Since human acts are under the direction of the will and man can only come to his destiny through human acts, the moral virtues are important in directing human conduct to its final goal. Moral virtue gives man a readiness to act in accord with reason and that which is reasonable leads man to his destiny: God.

There are as many specifically different moral virtues as there are specifically different moral acts. Hence there are many moral virtues but these may be reduced to four basic virtues which are called cardinal from the Latin term "cardo" meaning "hinge." All the other virtues, so to speak, hinge on four main virtues: prudence, justice, temperance and fortitude. This division is made in accord with the subjects of virtue, namely, the reason, the will, the concupiscible faculty and the irascible faculty. St. Thomas explains:

> For there are four subjects of the virtue we speak of now: viz., the power which is rational in its essence, and this is perfected by prudence; and that which is rational by participation, and is threefold, the will, subject of justice, the concupiscible faculty, subject of temperance, and the irascible faculty, subject of fortitude.[11]

1. The Intellect. If a person acts well, the will must first be illumined by the intellect presenting a true good to it. The intellect must be habituated to distinguish what is truly good from what is only apparently good in the circumstances of life. The intellect equipped with the virtue of discerning the reasonable thing to do in the particular circumstances of life, possesses the virtue of prudence.

2. The Will. A person naturally seeks the good but the will requires a special habit to dispose one to respect the good of other persons and to act reasonably toward them. This is the virtue of justice.

3. The Concupiscible Faculty. In respect to oneself, one may be disordered in seeking ends by the passions, the movements

---

[11] S. *Theol.*, P. I-II, q. 61, a. 2.

of the sensible appetite as in matters of sex, eating, drinking. A good habit must be in the sensible appetite ordering it according to right reason in pursuit of the sensible goods. This virtue is called temperance.

4. **The Irascible Faculty.** In the irascible faculty the appetite is in pursuit of the good that is difficult to obtain and associated with dangers; another virtue is required to moderate this faculty in action and this is the virtue of fortitude.

A. **Prudence.** Prudence is the right reason of things to be done. It is the rectitude of discretion concerning proper goals in human conduct, and it is both a practical intellectual virtue and a moral virtue. Prudence is a rectitude of reason that orders the will in pursuit of ends. It strikes the mean between extremes not in a mathematical way but in a judicial way. It gives the mode and form to all the other moral virtues, striking the mean between extremes, so that in a suitable time and by apt means the other virtues are exercised.

By prudence confidence in God and fear of God are reconciled. A prudent person is not overly confident in God to the point of being passive in his own life, as if God does everything, which is presumption. At the same time he avoids desperation which is begotten from an exaggerated fear of God. Prudence guides a man in the circumstances of his moral life so that humility does not become pusillanimity, courage does not become recklessness, modesty avoids prudishness.

The moral virtue of prudence is attained by knowledge and by discipline of the will. Although it presupposes some knowledge, it is a virtue rooted in the right order of doing rather than merely knowing. A person unlearned in ethics, a person not well-endowed in intelligence can still be a person of prudence by the acquisition of self-mastery, the right order of doing things in using apt means to proper goals. The use of apt means alone is not constitutive of prudence. Thieves, liars, lustful people sometimes show a marked cleverness in choosing and using apt means but for evil ends. The clever man need not be the prudent man. Such cleverness is sometimes called "prudence of the flesh."

The vices opposed to prudence are through defect and excess. Imprudence is by defect and pertains to persons who fall short of prudence due to inconstancy in their actions or inconsideration of apt means to proper ends or due to sheer negligence on their part. Imprudence by excess arises in too great a solicitude for material things, which especially arises out of avarice. It must be clearly recognized that the terms "prudent" and "imprudent" as used by the ethician and as they ordinarily occur in the English language are not always the same in meaning. In our American way of life, we are sometimes prone to call a person prudent because he is resourceful in money matters, whereas from the ethical insight into such matters, the person may very well be imprudent due to too great a zeal for the material.

B. Justice. There is a twofold meaning common to justice. Firstly it may be taken in a general sense to signify one who keeps the law, wherefore a man is said to be just. In its specific sense as a moral virtue, justice is the moral virtue inclining the will to render to everyone his right according to some measure of equality. The elements of right and equality are important to the definition of justice.

When another virtue shares in some way in the definition of justice but not perfectly it is said to be a potential part of justice. For example, what is given as a gift to another out of the virtue of gratitude cannot be said to be given out of justice in the perfect sense because the receiver does not have a right to the gift, so that the donor must give as a matter of justice. The gift is given because it is the decent or fitting thing to do. Gratitude is a potential part of justice. The virtue of religion is also a potential part of justice because man can never render to God homage that is equal to what is due to the all good God. Virtues that are potential parts of justice lack the element of right or equality, which is necessary to the essence of justice.

The object of justice is all exterior acts ordained to another person. The subject of justice is the will, since a man it not just merely because he knows that something is due to another. He is just because he acts rightly to another, giving the other what is his due. Sometimes two persons can be considered to be morally one, and so in their dealing with one another there is not strict justice which demands exterior acts ordained to another. For example, if a father fails to provide for his child, the evil that he commits is not injustice strictly but a violation of the virtue of piety which governs the relation of parent to child.

Justice is divided into three kinds: (1) Commutative justice: the regulation of giving what is due according to some measure of equality of a part to a part, as one citizen of the community to another; (2) Social justice: the regulation of what is due according to some measure of equality of the part to the whole, as the citizen to the state. It is also known as legal or general justice. (3) Distributive justice: the regulation of what is due according to some measure of equality of the whole to the parts as the state to its citizens.

1. Commutative Justice. This comes from the Latin word *"commutatio"* which means "exchange." It is strict justice and concerns the rights and duties of persons toward each other as in the exchange of goods, services, abilities, money. This is exemplified in contracts. Commutative justice demands that the parties are adequately distinct and that an object or objects belongs to someone by right. Only commutative justice most strictly has the elements of justice. In social justice and in distributive justice the individual is not completely distinct from society.

An example of commutative justice is found in buying and selling between individual persons or moral persons as business firms. If a man contracts to sell a plot of land to another, he has the obligation to turn it over to the other and the right to receive a suitable price. There is an arithmetic equality in commutative justice. If the agreed price is $500, the seller is obliged to turn over his land for that price and the buyer to pay it.

Restitution is necessary for violations of commutative justice. The reason for commutative justice is to establish the right order of things so that each will have that to which he has a right. Hence if one possesses what belongs to another, the article must be returned to its rightful owner. Furthermore, if one is guilty of causing another's loss, reparation must be made, even if the guilty person is not now in possession of more than he should have. This pertains not only to external goods such as money and other material possessions but also to internal goods as intellectual and bodily integrity and also to intermediate goods such as a person's good name and esteem in the community. Gossipers are bound to restitution as are thieves, reckless drivers and so forth. Gossipers can effect this sometimes by an explicit apology to the person they have harmed and public denial of their charges, when the gossip has calumniated or lied about someone. In political campaigns when a candidate is calumniated in the press, the person responsible for such lies must retract them in the press.

2. Social Justice. This is the virtue that moves the individual of a community to promote the common good of that community. The community may be the family, the State, or the human race. Justice demands that the part give its share to the whole as in payment of taxes, performance of military service. A citizen is bound by legal justice to fight for his country, unless he is sincerely convinced in his conscience that the war is unjust. Social justice demands the reasonable subordination of the individual good to the common good.

Marriage has an intimate relation to social justice. The primary purpose of marriage is the preservation and welfare of society. Violations of the natural law governing marriage either by the use of the vital powers outside of marriage or the abuse of those powers in marriage as by artificial birth control, are evils against social justice. The view that morals in reference to sex are purely a personal affair fails to take into account the social consequences of promiscuity, especially evidenced in the historical facts of the decline of nations: the Roman Empire. Population control, when it is required for the common good, must respect the natural law. It should not merely consider the business cycle.

3. Distributive Justice. This is the moral virtue that inclines the person or persons governing a community to promote the social good of the individual. In the distribution of justice from the governing to the governed there is a distribution according to a geometric or proportional equality rather than arithmetical as in commutative justice. The distribution in distributive justice is according to the abilities of the governed and according to their needs. Dignities, rewards, jobs in civil service are not given out equally to all but in proportion to abilities, work performed and so forth.

Frequently violations of distributive justice are also violations of commutative justice and so restitution must be made.

For example, if the law requires that a civil service job be given to the highest marked examinee in an examination, an official fails against both distributive and commutative justice if he gives the job to a friend instead of the examinee who received the highest grade. The official must make restitution to the person who is wronged.

C. Temperance. Temperance is the moral virtue that regulates and moderates the concupiscible appetite. It is the virtue that gives moderation in sense pleasures. The principal pleasures of the senses are associated with food, drink and the sexual appetite. Bodily pleasures are so alluring that there is danger of excess in their use unless one is guided by the rule of reason.

Temperance, inasmuch as it inclines a person to be moderate in food, is called abstinence, and its contrary vice is gluttony; in respect to drink it is called sobriety and its contrary vice is drunkenness; in respect to the sexual appetite, it is chastity and its opposite vice is lust or impurity. Temperance observes the mean in all bodily pleasures.

Chastity is the moral virtue which moderates the inclinations of the sex appetite according to right reason. Chastity refers to abstention from all deliberate sexual actions until marriage. There is also chastity in marriage, which is the exclusion of anything against the proper use of the sexual powers as ordained by God in nature. There are many misconceptions concerning chastity in our times because there are many misconceptions of the meaning of human nature and the moral law. There are some who believe that so long as there is no violence attached to the uses of the sexual appetite, so long as people willfully engage in its use, no harm is done. What they forget is that morality is founded on human nature according to proper pursuit of proper ends. Man cannot remake nature, so to speak, to fit his lusts. There is a plan, an order in human nature, which if violated results in disorder both in the private worlds of people and in society.

The primary end of the sexual appetite, to which great pleasures are attached, is the procreation of the species, the continuation of the race. Reproduction is a good not primarily of the individual but of the human race. The pleasures of sex must follow nature's design. Nature demands that venereal pleasure be allowed only between two who are conjoined in legitimate matrimony. This is for the good of the offspring and also for the good of conjugal love. In conjugal love the sexual appetite is expressed in the use of the exchange of rights over one another's bodies given in the matrimonial contract.

Youth especially must recognize the need for a matured reasonable approach to the control of the sexual appetite. Too often chastity is viewed merely as a taboo or an outmoded custom in our fast-moving age. Parents are quite often to blame in failing to educate their offspring in chastity. As was pointed out prudity is not a virtue. In the absence of proper parental education and moral discipline in such matters youth is an easy prey to sensuality. The objective approach of ethics is highly valuable in youth guidance in teaching that the sexual appetite (as in the case of any appetite) must follow nature's plan. Man is not intelligible in terms of sex, but sex is intelligible in terms of man, in the very order of his human being.

The principle that no deliberate venereal pleasure is permitted outside of matrimony should not induce scruples. Venereal pleasures such as sexual emotions of a physical nature can be permitted at times without evil. This happens when a person does something as a remote cause of such emotions, if there is no grave danger of the consent of the will. For example, some venereal pleasure might inculpably arise in reading an ordinary love story that is not narrated in an erotic manner or in dating as in "mixers" at which one properly conducts oneself.

D. Fortitude. Fortitude is the moral virtue that inclines a person to be courageous in dangers so that a person is not thereby deterred from doing good. The evils contrary to this virtue are the extremes: timidity by defect and audacity by excess. Fortitude strikes the mean between these extremes. The man of fortitude on the one hand is not a timid soul and on the other he is not foolhardy in audacity or rashness.

Fear of itself is not repugnant to fortitude. Sometimes it is prudent to be afraid. Fortitude moderates our fear so that it does not become exaggerated, as in cowardice. The martyr who dies for the truth, the hero in battle who performs brave deeds, the man who suffers loss in business rather than join in the injustices of his competitors, these persons may fear the dangers about them and still have the virtue of fortitude, so long as such fear is moderated by right reason in action. In our own age perhaps the worst fear that grips many in a materialistic way of life is the excessive fear of death. It is so excessive that some cannot bear to endure the thought of it in incurable illnesses and so prefer suicide to get it over with.

Fortitude not only controls our fears but also our rashness. The brave person is not always the person who rushes into dangers to do what is right and just. Sometimes it is audacity or rashness to take action. Fortitude sometimes calls for long suffering to stand and endure dangers rather than to be hot-tempered. The Fabian policy of waiting for the proper circumstances to achieve the good in dangerous circumstances is certainly prudent as compared with rushing headlong into certain or probable ruin. This is of course true when one is not obliged to act immediately and when there is reasonable hope of better circumstances for action. Youth is especially impulsive and inclined to immediate action. Patience, constancy, and perseverance are parts of the virtue of fortitude.

Difficulties of daily occurrence excite some people to undue anger. Fortitude is required to moderate people of such irascible temperament. Aristotle keenly observes:

> Now hot-tempered people get angry quickly and with the wrong persons and at the wrong things and more than is right. ... By reason of excess choleric people are quick-tempered and ready to be angry with everything and on every occasion; whence their name. Sulky people are hard to appease and retain their anger long; for they repress their passions.[12]

Magnanimity is a special kind of fortitude that inclines a person to great deeds in circumstances of great honor or dishonor. It is sometimes an arduous task for a person bearing great honors to act rightly. The big executive and the statesman have many opportunities to test their virtue. Wealth and power can corrupt a man as history testifies. Arduous duties accompany great honors. Persons who come to high offices equipped with knowledge that befits their dignity but devoid of virtue

---

[12] *Ethics*, Bk. IV, 5, 1126a.

are in proximate occasions of evil. The great man should be prepared to accept great honors and to endure great dishonors in failures, in disloyalties, in the intrigues of men. This is too much to ask of many men.

Suggested Reading

Aristotle, *Nicomachean Ethics,* Bk. I, ch. 13 Bk VII, ch. 10.

St. Thomas Aquinas, *S. Theol.,* P. I-II, qq. 49-65. *On the Virtues,* translated by J. Reid, (Providence: Providence College Press, 1951).

W. Farrell, *Companion to the Summa,* Vol. II, ch. VIII to XI.

W. Gerhard, "The Intellectual Virtue of Prudence" in *The Thomist.* Vol. VIII (1945), pp. 413-456.

Questions

1. What is moral virtue? Explain the terms of the definition.

2. Name and define the virtues of the speculative intellect. What distinguishes moral virtues from the intellectual virtues?

3. Name and define the virtue of the practical intellect. Why is prudence both a moral and intellectual virtue?

4. Distinguish art and prudence. Is the clever business man the same as the morally prudent man?

5. What intellectual virtues are necessary to the moral virtues?

6. What is a cardinal virtue?

7. Name the cardinal virtues. In what faculty of man is each one subjected?

8. What is prudence? What vices are contrary to prudence?

9. What is the moral virtue of justice? Name and define the three kinds of justice.

10. What is temperance? What vices are contrary to temperance?

11. What is chastity?

    a. Does this virtue only refer to the unmarried state?

    b. What is the primary end of marriage?

12. What is a widespread contemporary error concerning chastity and social mores? Criticize this view.

13. Define Fortitude. What vices are contrary to fortitude?

14. Is fear always the same as timidity? Are bravery and boldness in face of danger always the same? Discuss your replies.

15. What is magnanimity? Discuss the virtue and the role it plays in the life of the great man, viz., the statesman.

CONCLUSION TO PART TWO: HUMAN CONDUCT

THE OBJECT of the Second Part of *General Ethics* is as St. Thomas observes: "... to consider human acts in order to know by what acts we may attain happiness."[13] We have seen in this study that the human act is any act done by man with knowledge and consent. There are acts elicited by the will and commanded acts which come under the dominion of the will. This is the area of human responsibility. The acts of man which pertain to the vegetative powers and to the sensitive powers, which are not elicited or commanded, are not included in human acts. A special study was made of acts that are indirectly voluntary which are involved in the principle of the twofold effect.

A careful division was made between acts that are nonvoluntary and acts that are involuntary, namely, acts that we do not will to perform and which are against our will. Such actions are sometimes completely involuntary and sometimes only in some respect involuntary. The involuntary acts were studied according to the causes: ignorance, fear, passion, violence and habit.

All human acts are moral. Morality is not an innate instinct, a sentimental feeling, a will to perform one's duty, a taboo or social mores determined by the group, or always a matter of man-made law. Morality is measured by human nature in respect to its proper natural goals and its ultimate goal which is the source of all human pursuit of the good, namely, God. Without this objective reference morality becomes a matter of subjective reference, a point of view, a fashion or sentimental preference. The morality of a human act is the standard or criterion of good and evil determined by the object, end and circumstances of a human act. The standard of morals is proximately given in the natural law, ultimately in the divine law, and manifestly in human conscience.

The moral virtues, operative habits of doing good, facilitate our pursuit of the good. The cardinal virtues of prudence,

---

[13] S. *Theol.*, P. I-II, q. 6, prologue.

justice, temperance and fortitude moderate human acts as the basic virtues of the moral life. These are the virtues upon which the other virtues hinge. Prudence is the most important of the virtues in that it strikes the mean between extremes, which is necessary for any virtue. There can be no proper pursuit of human destiny unless a person is first of all prudent. For human destiny is not extremes.

Part Three

Law

*"We have now to consider the extrinsic principle
of acts . . . the extrinsic principle moving to good
is God, Who . . . instructs us by means of His
law . . ."*

S. *Theol.*, P. I-II, q. 90, Prologue.

INTRODUCTION

THE CONCEPT of law and its divisions (chapter one) along with the study of conscience (chapter two), sanction and obligation (chapter three), merit and demerit (chapter four) crime and punishment (chapter five) right and duty (chapter six) comprise the third part of *General Ethics*. The study of the philosophy of morality would be incomplete without the exploration of these concepts.

The external principle of moral action is God. In divine law God gives man the norm, direction, content and sanction of moral action.[1] The directive and obligatory influence of divine law is set forth in the synthesis of St. Thomas following St. Augustine as rooted in the great plan of the universe founded in God's holiness and wisdom. All laws are derived from the divine government of the world.

In this grand exposition of law St. Thomas does no violence to human freedom. The dignity of man as a free, rational agent is respected throughout. It is precisely because man is free and rational that the eternal law is fulfilled with knowledge of the end in a free and conscious pursuit of the end.

---

[1] *S. Theol.*, P. I-II, qq. 90-108.

CHAPTER ONE

Law: The Obligation to Live Morally

I. THE CONCEPT OF LAW

ACCORDING to St. Thomas the term "law" originated from the word "to bind" because law obliges us to act.[2] In its improper sense law extends to the irrational order as when we speak of a law in physics or chemistry because a uniformity of action is observed and expressed in a formula as in Newton's laws of motion. Law in its proper sense is restricted to intelligent creatures, who can be obliged to act.

A human act is moral through its transcendental relation to the rule of morals. The rule is the law. It directs persons to act toward their ends by imposing the obligation to act on the free rational nature. St. Thomas defines law as "an ordinance of reason for the common good, promulgated by him who has the care of the community."[3]

Law is an ordinance of reason: an order or command of reason. Hence it is not a mere counsel, advice or suggestion to act. Law obliges a person to act. It is of the practical

---

[2] S. Theol., P. I-II, q. 90, a. 1.
[3] Ibid., a. 4.

reason ordained to act. It is a command of the legislator: e.g., the Congress in the United States. Although it is imposed by an act of the legislative authority's will, it is formulated by reason.[4] It must be reasonable. It should be consistent and not impose contradictory obligations. It should be just, respecting higher rights and distributing duties with equity. It should be observable and therefore not unreasonably harsh. It should be enforceable; otherwise, only good people will observe it. Finally it should be useful by serving the community in some way.

Law is for the common good. By this end it is distinguished from commands or precepts given only to individuals for some personal good. The law has for its final cause the good of the community as a whole. This does not formally mean the greatest good of the greatest number. The common good is not a sum arrived at by counting up individuals. It is determined by what pertains to the end of the society as a society. Individuals are born and die but the common good remains throughout. Law is an ordination firm and stable. It endures unless repealed by the proper authority, when this is possible. It is at least relatively perpetual. When laws are founded on our very nature as the moral law that obliges us to honor God, they cannot be repealed. There is no such thing as permission to be exempt from natural law, for example, permission to practice artificial birth control.

Law is promulgated by him who has the care of the community.[5] Promulgation means making the law known to those who are obliged to keep it. This does not mean that each and every subject necessarily knows the law. The law is published in such a way that the subjects can know it without great difficulty. The manner of publication depends on the circumstances. In the modern state the media of communication offer the means for efficient, widespread promulgation of laws. Once promulgated law binds objectively even though one is unaware of it. Such a person can be excused by reason of invincible ignorance. Civil law usually does not

---

[4] S. Theol., P. I-II, q. 90, a. 3.
[5] Ibid., q. 97, a. 3, a. 4.

accept the plea of invincible ignorance. It is often difficult to prove that the person so attesting is not lying.

A law must be made by a lawgiver who has jurisdiction. Jurisdiction is the right to impose or administer law. It pertains to the authority of a legitimate superior, a physical person such as a monarch or a moral person as a congress or parliament.

This definition of law pertains not only to civil law but also to ecclesiastical law. It pertains not only to man-made laws but also to law decreed by God in nature and in His revelation. God is the supreme lawgiver Who has care of the whole community of creation and Who makes laws and promulgates them for the common good of all for His glory.

From this definition it is evident that law is not given to hinder human liberty but rather to guide it. For the end of law is to direct human acts for the common good which redounds to the good of the individual. Law guides man in his moral life in achieving his proper goals. The imperfections of man in his present state strengthens the need for law. Certainly whatever aids man in achieving his goals perfects his liberty, which is founded in rational nature. The unlawful, unreasonable man is not the truly free man. Liberty is not license to do what one likes. The proper observance of rights and duties demands the rule of law.

Law can be divided by reason of origin:
- Eternal
- Temporal
  - Natural
  - Positive
    - Divine
    - Human
      - Ecclesiastical
      - Civil

Divine positive law such as is given in revelation, the ecclesiastical law as in the code of Canon Law are not within the scope of the philosopher's inquiry in General Ethics.

II. ETERNAL LAW

St. Thomas explains eternal law:

> ... granted that the world is governed by divine providence... the whole community of the universe is governed by the divine reason. Therefore the very notion of the government of things in God, the ruler of the

universe, has the nature of a law. And since the divine reason's conception of things is not subject to time, but is eternal ... this kind of law must be called eternal.[6]

The eternal law is the rule of divine wisdom, which is eternal, ordering all things to their end. It is demonstrated in Theodicy that God is personal and that He provides for creatures. The rule of divine wisdom whereby He provides for creatures from eternity is called the eternal law. The existence of such law is founded on the divine attribute of wisdom in God. God directs creatures to Himself, Who is the Highest Good of all.

The eternal law is not the same as divine providence. Divine providence is a consequence of God's eternal law. Providence is the execution of the eternal law in individual creatures.[7] The eternal law is not knowable by man in itself since it is in divine wisdom but it can be known somewhat by man in its effects. All creatures are subject to the eternal law. This pertains to both the physical and the moral order because God ordains all for His glory.

III. THE NATURAL LAW

Natural law is the participation of the eternal law in rational nature. This participation is twofold: through natural inclinations in man and through the first principles of practical reason. The first principles of practical reason are the rational expression of natural inclinations. They constitute natural law. This is not the same as saying that natural law is rational nature itself because rational nature can be the subject of good or evil. In other words rational nature can conform or not conform to the natural law. Furthermore, to say that rational nature is natural law would be to make a man a law unto himself.

> ... (rational nature) has a share of the Eternal Reason, whereby it has a natural inclination to its proper act and end: and *this participation of the eternal law in the rational creature is called the natural law.*[8]

God promulgates the natural law to man through his rational nature. It is written so to speak in our very beings. By this

---

[6] S. *Theol.*, P. I-II, q. 91, a. 1.
[7] St. Thomas Aquinas, *On Truth*, q. 5, aa. 1 and 6.
[8] S. *Theol.*, P. I-II, q. 91, a. 2.

is not meant, however, that man is born with innate ideas of right and wrong. Man's nature is rational and he discovers the natural law by the light of natural reason in drawing conclusions about his nature. By self reflection and by observing the conduct of his fellow-men he can estimate what is natural and what is unnatural, what is proper in action according to natural ends and what is not. There are first principles of the practical reason which guide his reasoning. They are called first not because they are inborn but because one is naturally disposed to know them in natural inclinations.

The existence of the natural law is proved by St. Thomas in the following passage:

> Law being a rule and measure can be in a person in two ways: in one way, as in him that rules and measures; in another way, as in that which is ruled and measured. ... Therefore, since all things subject to divine providence are ruled and measured by the eternal law ... it is evident that all things partake in some way in the eternal law, insofar as, namely, from its being imprinted on them, they derive their respective inclinations to their proper acts and ends. Now among all others, the rational creature is subject to divine providence in a more excellent way, insofar as it itself partakes of a share of providence, by being provident both for itself and others. Therefore, it has a share of the eternal reason whereby it has a natural inclination to its proper act and end: and this participation of the eternal law in the rational creature is called the natural law.... The light of natural reason, whereby we discern what is good and what is evil, which is the function of the natural law, is nothing else than an imprint on us of the divine light.[9]

In the eternal law God decrees that all creatures attain their proper end by proper acts. This is true of man. By the light of natural reason man discerns God's plan in his nature through his natural inclinations toward his proper ends. Experience also testifies that man is obliged to follow his natural inclinations as the norm of his acts toward what is good.

1. THE KNOWLEDGE OF THE NATURAL LAW. It is evident that all men do not agree to everything that is good or evil according to their knowledge of natural inclinations. There are primitive

---

[9] *S. Theol.*, P. I-II, q. 91, a. 2.

tribes whose code of human conduct affirms polygamy as a good. There are civilized people whose moral code condones divorce, mercy-killing, sterilization and other evils. In the Wolfenden report on public morals made in England in September, 1957 the terms "natural" and "unnatural" were avoided because the committee did not want to patronize any one school of thought on such matters. The term "natural law" is nowadays taken by some as an authoritarian point of view.

It is evident that all the principles of the natural law are not known in the same way by all people. The reason is that they are in various grades of importance according to nature. We note three principal divisions: 1) Primary principle: do good and avoid evil, 2) Moral axioms: as do not steal. 3) Remote conclusions: as "Artificial birth control is wrong." St. Thomas explains:

> There belongs to natural law, first, certain most general precepts that are known to all; and secondly, certain secondary and more detailed precepts, which are, as it were, conclusions following closely from first principles. As to these general principles, the natural law, in the abstract, can nowise be blotted out from men's hearts. But it is blotted out in the case of a particular action, insofar as reason is hindered from applying the general principle to the particular action because of concupiscence or some other passions. But as to the other, i.e., the secondary precepts, the natural law can be blotted out from the human heart either by evil persuasions, just as in speculative matters errors occur in respect of necessary conclusions; or by vicious customs and corrupt habits, as, among some men, theft, and even unnatural vices . . . were not esteemed sinful.[10]

The more common or universal the principle, the more impossible it is to be unknown. The more particular and determinate, the more possible it is for one to be ignorant or to be deceived in its knowledge. We distinguish three orders of principles in the natural law. The primary moral principle, the universal moral axioms of principles, and remote, reasoned conclusions.

The primary moral principle is known to all. It is impossible to have invincible ignorance of it.

---

10 S. *Theol.*, P. I-II, q. 94, a. 6.

... the first precept of law, *that good is to be done and pursued, and evil is to be avoided.* All other precepts of the natural law are based upon this; so that all the things which the practical reason naturally apprehends as man's good (or evil) belong to the precepts of the natural law under the form of things to be done or avoided.[11]

This first principle of the practical reason is founded on the notion of good: good is that which all things seek. It is self-evident.[12] It can be phrased in a variety of ways such as "Do good and avoid evil"; "Live according to right reason"; "Seek your destiny," and so forth.

There are other general principles based on this first principle. These follow from the first principle in some way. They are called moral axioms, such as "Adore God," "Do not murder," "Do not steal," "Do not lie." There is no invincible ignorance of these general principles in the abstract in persons who have reached the age of reason and reason normally. However, vicious customs and corrupt practices can induce errors whereby such things as murder, theft and unnatural vices are esteemed by some people as good. This can take effect among the educated. A philosophy of morality can itself be false, such as the teaching of the superman beyond the good and evil of ordinary men as propounded by Friedrich Nietzsche and his sister Elizabeth.

Remote conclusions of the natural law inferred from the general principles can be invincibly unknown to people. One can err in drawing these conclusions as one can err in other forms of argumentation due to defects in education, biases, passion and so forth. For example, one can err in believing that artificial birth control is a good because of the overpopulation of a community, or the poverty of a family. One can err in believing that divorce is good when a married couple have lost their love for one another. One can err in believing that sterilization of the feeble minded is a good for the community.

Finally men can err in applying moral principles to a particular case. One can know the principles of the natural law in the abstract and still err in applying the principles in concrete cases due to human frailties. Innocent men have been hanged, imprisoned, exiled due to errors of judgment in wrongly apply-

---

[11] S. *Theol.*, P. I-II, q. 94, a. 2.
[12] *Ibid.*

ing right moral principles. Individuals can misjudge their own actions as well as others. One can estimate virtue where there is really vice, or vice where there is virtue. This can be caused by the inability to use right principles correctly rather than any viciousness toward others.

2. THE PROPERTIES OF THE NATURAL LAW. There are four basic properties of the natural law: it is one essentially, it is immutable, it is the same for all, and it is indelibly written in the heart of man.

It is essentially one because all the precepts of the natural law are founded on the first precept: do good and avoid evil.

A. THE NATURAL LAW IS UNCHANGEABLE. Change can be by addition or by subtraction. Our concern here is with change by subtraction of moral precepts from the natural law. We shall consider additions to the natural law made by human positive law at the end of this chapter. In respect to the general principles or moral axioms, the natural law is unchangeable such as "Do not murder," "Tell the truth." As regards remote and detailed conclusions from the general principles of the practical reason, in most cases these are unchangeable but in some cases they are changeable. For example, in most cases, goods held in trust must be returned to their rightful owners but there are circumstances where it would be injurious and unreasonable to restore them. A gun should not be restored to a man who has become drunk or violently angered. If goods held in trust are claimed in wartime by citizens of an enemy nation, they can be rightfully withheld.[13]

B. THE NATURAL LAW IS THE SAME FOR ALL. The natural law is the same for all in respect to the primary and general principles and as regards the remote conclusions in most cases but in some there are exceptions, as was stated above. There is not a natural law for primitives and another for the civilized. The natural law is the same for all man according to its rectitude, which is founded in our common rational nature. When circumstances vary so that right reason demands an exception for the sake of right order in nature, there is no contradiction of the ordinary proper principles but rather a change in the matter. All the principles of the natural law are founded on the right

---

[13] *S. Theol.*, P. I-II, q. 94, a. 4.

order of things. Remote conclusions may not be known to all but they are objectively the same precepts for all by nature.

C. THE INDELIBILITY OF THE NATURAL LAW IN THE HEART OF MAN. All men endowed with reason know the primary principle (do good and avoid evil) and the moral axioms as universal principles of morality. Remote detailed conclusions and also right applications of the moral principles may be blotted out from the hearts of men by depraved customs, by passion and so forth. The killing of the aged and incurable among some primitives in their wretched life in the jungle is not regarded by them as an act of murder but as mercy killing. So too modern pagans in civilized countries sometimes kill the incurable and regard this not as an act of murder but as "mercy killing." We are sometimes too apt to judge depraved customs as proper to primitive people. Our modern world has become engrossed in many depraved customs practiced sometimes by the highly educated elite, espousing false theories of morality propagated to the general public under the guise of "science," "education," "culture."

Lu K'uan (1538-1618), a Chinese philosopher of the Ming dynasty, presents a significant insight into the indelibility of the natural law (called *T'ien lei* or *lei* in Chinese):

> There are two things supreme in this world: one is *lei*, the other is political authority. Of the two, *lei* is more supreme. When *lei* is discussed in the Imperial Court or Palace, even the Emperor cannot suppress it by his authority. And even when *lei* is suppressed temporarily, it will always triumph in the end and will prevail in the world throughout the ages.[14]

In contemporary times the inability of some to grasp the proper meaning of natural law lies in their belief that "human nature," as indeed every universal concept, is merely a common name. The failure to appreciate the abstraction of universal essence from things is at the root of the difficulty. This relativism of nominalism in human knowledge prevents the proper understanding of natural law, which is founded in the natural inclinations that follow from the species "rational animal." These

---

[14] Lu K'uan, "Groaning Words" quoted by Hu Shih in his "Natural Law in the Chinese Tradition" *University of Notre Dame Natural Law Institute Proceedings*, V (1953) 152.

critics of the natural law are amazed that one can speak of moral precepts founded on human nature for all times and in all places.

The metaphysical foundation of the natural law is to be complemented with inductive studies of mankind as evidenced in sociology and anthropology. The important data gathered by experts in these fields enables us to know of the natural law found in peoples. The methods of these sciences, however, presuppose a basic knowledge of the meaning of man and man as a moral being. False philosophies of man and morality can introduce, as indeed they have introduced, false apriorisms such as the belief that some primitives had no morals without sufficiently investigating the mores of the primitive tribes.

3. THE NATURAL LAW HAS NO DISPENSATIONS. There are no dispensations or exemptions from the natural law any more than one can naturally expect a dispensation from the law of gravity while walking on a slippery pavement. There is more reason for no dispensation in the former than in the latter (which could occur by a miracle which is apart from the natural course of things). A dispensation from the natural law would imply a dispensation from one's human nature, which is essential to one's very being. One cannot obtain a dispensation whereby murder, the unjust taking of another's life, becomes a moral good. One cannot obtain a dispensation whereby the use of artificial forms of contraception are morally good since this is against the natural function of the vital powers in man.

Legitimate practice of the rhythm is not a *permission* for artificial birth control. It is simply observing nature's unfertile periods with a just cause such as financial limitations of a family. The taking of pills to normalize infertile periods in women with irregular cycles is not making use of "birth control pills," when their intention is not to prevent birth but to normalize their cycle. The use of such pills in women who have legitimate reason for practicing rhythm is not against nature as indeed artificial birth control is.

In October, 1959, the report of a study group of the World Council of Churches affirmed that the world population 'explosion' made it imperative for parents everywhere to engage in effective family planning. The report commented that there is no moral difference between various methods of preventing conception. In the light of the natural law, however, the means of preventing conception make a great deal of difference. It is conceded that there are many circumstances in which family limitation is permissible but no circumstance in which it is right morally to have intercourse while destroying deliberately the physical integrity of the marriage act. Artificial contraception is always morally wrong. The use of the sterile period, on the other hand, is essentially different because it does not destroy the integrity of the marriage act but leaves it intact.

One cannot remake human nature, so to speak. Human nature is an entity essentially given in nature. As Author of nature, God wills that we live according to the nature that He created. If God changed the natural law, He would will otherwise, which would be a contradiction. This is impossible in God. Consequently natural law is unchangeable both on the part of God and on the part of human nature. This does not mean that man cannot improve on nature by inventions. It means that such changes must respect human nature in its natural order. When eyeglasses were first invented some people falsely protested that they were unnatural. So too there are people who regard medicine as an unnatural evil thing.

When we spoke of exemptions in respect to the general principles of the natural law, we did not mean that these principles are changed in themselves but only that *the matter or circumstances is changed* so that other principles apply in these circumstances. The change is not in the form of the general principle itself that applies for the greater number of cases but in the matter which requires other principles in some cases.

IV. HUMAN POSITIVE LAW

Human Positive law is defined as the ordination of human reason through the mode of a conclusion or determination deduced from the natural law and conforming to it for the common good promulgated by him who has the care of the community.[15] The lawgiver may be a human person as a king

[15] S. *Theol.*, P. I-II, q. 91, a. 3, a. 95, a. 2.

or a moral person (or judicial person) as a congress or parliament. The civil law is the human positive law of a state.

Human positive law is derived from the natural law in two ways. Firstly it is derived by way of conclusion from a general principle of the natural law such as laws against perjury are derived from the natural law concerning telling the truth. Secondly a human positive law can be derived from the natural law as a determination which is not given in the natural law, such as determining the kind of penalty to be attached to perjury or some other crime.[16]

Man needs to make laws for the good of society and for his own good not because the natural law is defective. The natural law is good insofar as it goes. However, it was never intended by the Creator to be the only law operative in human affairs. The very nature of man shows the need for man-made laws. This need may be summed up in the following four reasons:

(1) Some precepts of the natural law may be obscured in some people. As we have noted all the precepts of the natural law are not known to all men. There are people who either lack the knowledge of some of the moral precepts of the natural law or their application. These people cannot simply be left to nature, so to speak. They must not only be informed about the moral precepts of which they are ignorant but also enforced to obey them insofar as this pertains to the common good of the community.

(2) The natural law does not always give sufficient sanctions in this world for violations of the law. Experience testifies that the thief is not sanctioned by nature so that he is penalized for a crime committed. There is need for a man-made penal code and execution of penalties for violators.

(3) The natural law often allows a choice of possible means to an end. In social action a definite means is necessary or at times the better thing toward acquiring needed ends. For example, the natural law decrees that man must preserve life. There are many ways of preserving life. In factories, however, the natural law does not clearly prescribe the safety measures for workers. Legislation is required for the preservation of the

---

[16] S. *Theol.*, P.I-II, q. 95, a. 2.

life of the workers as in machine shops. The machines must be adequately equipped so as not to injure workers.

(4) Complex and changing social life requires man-made laws. The precepts of the natural law demand interpretation in the light of social phenomena in the world of man. The relation of man to man in the circumstances of commerce and industry, human welfare in general in the changes of history require up-to-date laws. The natural law which is the same for all men in all places and ages was not meant to suffice for such details. Providence has left such natural considerations to human law. Hence we have labor laws considering the rights and duties of workers and management, copyright laws, admiralty law for the seas, international law. As man enters the regions of "outer space" there will be needed laws to direct rights and duties for man on the moon and other places in the heavens.

1. INTERNATIONAL LAW AND THE LAW OF NATIONS. Positive law is exemplified in the civil laws of our federal government, the laws of a State of the Union, the municipal law. Another example is international law which declares the rules for nations in their relations with one another. Modern international law owes a great deal to the work of Francis de Vitoria (1480-1546) who attempted to codify existing customs and apply them to nations in their relations. After the reformation in the sixteenth century Hugo Grotius in his work *The Rights of War and Peace* contributed greatly to the modern concept of international law. The United Nations is a present-day attempt to regulate the conduct of nations by international justice. Unfortunately nationalistic interests often hinder its progress.

The great law makers of the West were the Romans. They were presented with the difficulty of solving cases involving Roman citizens and persons belonging to subject nations of the vast Roman Empire. The Romans attempted to solve the difficulty by taking the common denominator of the customs and laws of the nations. This was called the *law of nations or ius gentium*. After the dissolution of the Roman empire the nations continued to use this law of nations in forming their laws. St. Thomas quotes the Roman jurist Gaius:

> whatever natural reason decrees among all men, is observed by all equally and is called the law of nations.[17]

---

[17] S. *Theol.*, P. II-II, q. 57, a. 3, ad 1.

Private property, for example, results from the natural law. However, as an institution of men, private property is of the law of nations. The actual distribution of property is not by natural law. Nature as such does not give a man a title to this parcel of land, although man's natural needs require private property. The institution of private property in the actual distribution of possessions is of the law of nations. It is common to the nations.[18] The *division* of possession is not according to the natural law but rather arose from human agreement which belongs to positive law... the ownership of possessions is not contrary to the natural law but an addition thereto devised by human reason.[19] Communism is against this requirement founded on nature by actually making the state, i.e., the dictator or the top party leaders, the sole owner of things.

2. POPULAR ACCEPTANCE AND CIVIL LAW. Popular acceptance is not necessary for civil laws except when the mode of government is that of a democracy. Democracy is the rule of the people, such as in some cantons of Switzerland where people vote for these laws in a public forum. Popular acceptance also holds for laws that require a popular referendum. In a republic such as the United States where a governing body is selected by the voters, the laws are made by the congress to whom the people have given the authority. All authority comes from God ultimately and proximately from the people. The people may give this authority to one man as in a dictatorship or monarchy or they may give it to a governing body such as a congress as in a republic. The mere refusal of a people to obey a law does not constitute its illegality. The refusal of the people to obey the law may of course indicate its unreasonableness, which would disqualify it as a law. The mere fact of refusal by the people to obey, however, does not disqualify a law. Furthermore, a proper legislator or legislative body may tacitly allow a law to go unobserved, which is equivalent to its repeal. A true law, however, cannot be removed except by repeal which is explicit or tacit by the proper authority.

3. INTERPRETATION OF CIVIL LAW. Civil laws are generally interpreted best by reasonable custom. St. Thomas explains the juridical value of custom:

---

18 S. *Theol.*, P. II-II, q. 57, a. 3.
19 *Ibid.*, q. 66, a. 2, ad 1.

> Wherefore by actions also, if they be repeated, so as to make custom, law can be changed and expounded, and also something can be established which obtains force of law, insofar as by repeated external actions, the inward movement of the will, and concepts of reason are most effectually declared; for when a thing is done again and again, it seems to proceed from a deliberate judgment of reason. Accordingly custom has the force of a law, abolishes law, and is the interpreter of law.[20]

The meaning of a law is easily understood by the usual manner in which it is carried out in the lives of subjects. Custom of course must have at least the tacit approval of the lawgiver, the person or legal body that makes the laws. The lawgiver has the right to interpret the meaning of the law or it may be given by jurists of authority. In our nation the Supreme Court decides on interpretation of the law.

Custom, however, must be reasonable in the interpretation of law. In many communities in the United States segregation of Negroes from Whites is pleaded by reason of long standing custom. Although change from established custom must be prudent, it must be stated that this custom of segregation is unnatural; it is against reason.

False interpretations of the law by custom should be reprobated by the lawgiver. By tacit approval of the lawgiver custom may not only interpret but also establish or abolish a law. Rigorous interpretation of the law to the letter which is devoid of the spirit of the law is generally safeguarded against by interpretation by custom. Human nature is not inclined to rigorous interpretation. Laws are made for human beings and not automatons.

Unreasonable hardship or impossibility of observance excuses a person from keeping a civil law. Such human laws are expected to be reasonable but it is unreasonable to expect a person to observe a civil law if it is impossible or subjects one to excessive hardships. Invincible ignorance excuses one from observing the law in conscience but the civil authority is not expected to accept every plea of invincible ignorance. It is difficult to give evidence for such ignorance in some circumstances and the civil authority must judge on evidence presented.

---

[20] S. *Theol.*, P. I-II, q. 97, a. 3.

4. OBEDIENCE AND UNJUST LAWS: Some unjust laws are passed by legislative bodies of the civil authority which are directly against the natural law. For example, laws against man's duty to honor God through the virtue of religion exist in the Soviet dictatorship. Such a law which dictates something intrinsically wrong must be disobeyed. Such "laws" are not really laws but rather evil commands which must be opposed by the reasonable means available. If the only reasonable means is revolution then the people have the right to rise against such an unnatural system of law as imposed by the Communist State. However, there must be some reasonable hope of the revolution succeeding. The sad case of the Hungarians dims such hopes on the modern scene of the Iron Curtain world.

Unjust laws that do not require a person to do something intrinsically evil may be tolerated. It is never permitted to do what is intrinsically evil but one may suffer injustice. Such laws may be resisted or obeyed according to prudence. For example, the unreasonably low wages decreed to be paid to the Hungarian workers by the Satellite government in Hungary could be accepted as a matter of expediency by the workers. One may yield a lesser right to avoid greater evils that can come in scandal or disturbance.[21]

Suggested Reading

St. Thomas Aquinas, *S. Theol.*, I-II, qs. 90-108.

H. Romnen, *The Natural Law* (St. Louis: Herder Co., 1948).

Natural Law and the Legal Profession (Chicago: Catholic Lawyers Guild: 1950).

S. Sieber and F. Mueller, *Social Life of Primitive Man* (Techny, Illinois: Mission Press, 1950).

F. LeBuffe and J. Hayes, *The American Philosophy of Law* (N.Y.: Jesuit Educational Association, 1953).

Questions

1. Define law and explain the terms of the definition.
2. What is the function of law in relation to morality?
3. What is the eternal law? Prove there is an eternal law.
4. What is the natural law? Prove there is a natural law.
5. What are the three kinds of principles given in the natural law? Discuss the knowledge of these principles in all men.
6. State and explain the four properties of the natural law.

---

[21] *S. Theol.*, P. I-II, q. 96, a. 4.

7. Why do some educated people in our times find it difficult to profess belief in the natural law?

8. Explain the statement: "The Natural law has no dispensations." Illustrate this principle.

9. What is human positive law?

10. Give four reasons why there is need for human positive law. Explain these reasons.

11. What is international law? Discuss the United Nations and the use of international law.

12. What is the law of nations?

13. How is civil law derived from the natural law?

14. How are civil laws to be interpreted?

15. When must citizens disobey unjust laws? When may they disobey unjust laws?

Conscience

I. CONSCIENCE

CONSCIENCE IS OFTEN considered to be a kind of interior feeling that a person has concerning good and evil in guiding one's conduct. This erroneous view is associated with the rather commonplace sentimentalism that good and evil depends upon one's personal feelings of the pleasant and unpleasant in life. Actually the less feeling and the more intelligence there is in conscience, the more it is inclined to be true in guiding us in the circumstances of life.

Law, as we have seen, contains the universal precepts of the moral life. It obliges us to act morally in the light of these universal precepts. But this is not enough for guiding a person in the concrete circumstances of life. There must be some application of principles to the concrete circumstances. It is not enough that a person knows that lying as such is wrong. One must know further that this particular act constitutes a lie. Conscience is defined as the judgment of the practical reason concerning an individual act to be a good to be done or an evil to be avoided. St. Thomas affirms:

For conscience is said to witness, to bind, or incite but also to accuse, torment or rebuke. And all these follow the application of knowledge or science to what we do. . . .[1]

Conscience is referred to as the subjective norm of morality because it is in the knowing subject as opposed to the objective norms: the eternal law and the natural law. It is not a special faculty of the soul. Its function is adequately explained by the act of the intellect in judging in individual moral cases. There are of course emotional factors involved in making an act of conscience. These do not constitute the essence of conscience. They may accompany an act of conscience.

II. ANALYSIS OF THE JUDGMENT OF CONSCIENCE

1. An abstract moral principle.
2. Applied to a concrete situation.
3. Conclusion: a judgment of conscience.

In our everyday experience we are frequently making judgments of conscience as to what we ought to do and what we ought to avoid doing. Some ethicians give a great deal of attention to what is called the language of morals. This is often nothing else than the study of conscience in action. Unfortunately these studies such as Ray Lepley edited in *The Language of Value* do not adequately understand the subjective and objective norms of morality.[2] They fail to interpret the phenomena under study in the light of a true science of ethics.

Judgments of conscience follow the general laws of reasoning. They are either true or false judgments. In every judgment of conscience which is a conclusion of a form of reasoning, there is at least implied a major and a minor premise. The major premise contains some universal moral precept. It is in the order of the fundamental, universal, moral principles, which is sometimes called *synderesis*—the habit of universal moral principles. The major premise may be a fundamental, universal, moral principle itself or include such a principle, such as "Do not murder" or "Do not make a direct attack on the fetus" which includes the universal law against murder. The minor

---

[1] *S. Theol.*, P. I, q. 79, a. 13.
[2] Ray Lepley, editor *The Language of Value* (N.Y.: Columbia University Press, 1957).

premise states a particular act in its concrete circumstances which falls under the major premise such as: The taking of this drug produces a direct attack on the fetus in these circumstances. The conclusion: "I must not use this drug here and now" is a judgment of conscience.

It is apparent that we are not always aware of major and minor premises in making judgments of conscience. Reflection, however, shows that there is always some basic principle, true or false, which guides us in moral judgments concerning concrete cases. Even in emotional or sentimental biases that lead us falsely to moral conclusions we can detect major principles. The person who has a false conscience concerning artificial birth control may reason, "This is right because we cannot afford another child." The major principle here is that inadequate financial conditions justify artificial birth control. Emotional bias toward material welfare and fear of sacrifice can enter greatly into these judgments of conscience.

III. THE KINDS OF CONSCIENCE

A. ANTECEDENT AND CONSEQUENT CONSCIENCE: Conscience can refer to future actions or to past actions. When conscience refers to future acts it is called antecedent conscience. We make a judgment of conscience before we undertake some action. When conscience refers to past actions it is called consequent conscience. When we examine our conscience as to the moral good or evil of our acts already committed, this is an exercise of consequent conscience. Antecedent conscience is practically more important inasmuch as it is moral reflection before action, which can guide us to doing good and avoiding evil in our lives. Its acts are chiefly four in kind: to command to act when one should, to forbid action when it is evil, to persuade or to permit when there is choice between the better and the worse and there is no obligation to act, or to abstain from action.

B. TRUE OR ERRONEOUS CONSCIENCE: Reasoning can be true or erroneous and so conscience as an act of reasoning can be true or false. A true conscience is one that judges to be good what is really good and to be evil what is really deprived of its proper good. An erroneous conscience fails to judge objectively what is good and evil. It judges the good to be evil as in the case of a scrupulous conscience or it judges the evil to be good as in the case of a lax conscience.

C. VINCIBLY AND INVINCIBLY ERRONEOUS CONSCIENCE: All error involves ignorance and ignorance can be vincible or invincible. A vincibly erroneous conscience can be corrected by prudent means. For example, if a Catholic doctor is in doubt about the morality of a certain hysterectomy case, he can easily contact the Catholic Chaplain of the hospital to dispel error. In fact he is obliged to consult a competent moralist insofar as he is aware of doubts in moral matters for the sake of true knowledge.

An invincibly erroneous conscience cannot be corrected by prudent means. For example, a doctor in a Soviet Union hospital believes erroneously that any hysterectomy is legitimate, if the government endorses it. He has no prudent means of correcting his conscience in his pagan surroundings.

A person is obliged to correct a vincibly erroneous conscience. For example, the scrupulous conscience ought to be corrected by prudent means with the help of sound direction from a prudent person and by self-discipline especially of the imagination. The vivid imagination of the scrupulous person can give rise to neurotic anxieties over imaginary evils. Scrupulosity is not a sign of virtue. All the virtues are governed by the first cardinal virtue, prudence.

D. CERTAIN AND DOUBTFUL CONSCIENCE: Conscience can be certain or doubtful. A certain conscience judges that an act is good or evil without fear that the opposite is true. A conscience is doubtful when judgment is suspended because a person has good reasons for both sides or no good reason for either side. A person is in doubt between the law and liberty. Is he free or bound to act in a given situation? He is uncertain whether or not he is bound to some obligation.

E. GENERAL PRINCIPLES OF CONSCIENCE: There are two general principles governing judgments of conscience. (1) Always obey a certain conscience. (2) Never act with a doubtful conscience. By a certain conscience is not necessarily meant a true conscience. A certain conscience can be true or erroneous. Certain conscience at least implies that subjectively a person has no prudent fear of the opposite being true in a judgment of conscience. It suffices that a man is prudently satisfied that from what he knows of things morally, he is doing the right thing. A person who is certain that a war is unjust is obliged to be a conscientious objector. A person who is certain that the Christian religion is the true religion is obliged to become a Christian. A person with a certain conscience, who is subjectively convinced that something ought to be done or to be avoided, is obliged to act even though his conscience is erroneous. Such a person believes that he is acting for the perfective good. One must follow a certain conscience. There remains, however, the duty to correct an erroneous conscience whenever one can prudently do so.

F. CONSCIENCE AND RELIGION: These principles of conscience are especially important in man's duty of religion. There are many people who have a certain conscience that a false religion is true. They do not recognize their religion as false. They are obliged to follow their certain conscience. But this is not the same as saying that what is false has the right to exist (objective right). Man cannot force reality to follow his subjective convictions, no matter how firm one may assent to them. False religions have no objective rights as such as far as natural law is concerned. However, persons in error concerning religious beliefs have the right in their certain consciences to follow what they believe to be true in a private profession of belief.

In the pluralism of modern society especially here in America there are hundreds of religious creeds publicly professed. In a great deal of ethical theories there is a purely subjectivist approach to religious differences, which leaves one with the attitude that religion is merely a matter of private conscience dependent upon one's point of view in such matters. In respecting the principle that one must always follow a certain conscience, one must also keep in mind man's duty to objective evidence, to correct an erroneous conscience. Also, an erroneous conscience does not give one the right to injure others, physically or spiritually. For example, the state has the right to order a blood transfusion for a child requiring it, when parents refuse to allow it out of false religious principles. Conscience as a judgment of the practical reason is bound to objective evidence. Contradictory religious creeds cannot both be true. There is a duty to serve the one true God in truth. A person must strive not only for a certain conscience but also for a true conscience in all matters.

When a person has an erroneous conscience in religious matters, it is important to consider whether the error is vincible or invincible. A vincibly erroneous conscience cannot be a certain conscience. A conscience is vincibly erroneous in religious matters when one can prudently correct it by adhering to the true religion. This implies on the part of the person that he realizes that he is in error or at least that he is doubtful about his assent and should consider the objective truth of religious belief.

IV. THE REFLEX PRINCIPLES: PROBABILISM AND EQUIPROBABILISM

In the case of a doubtful conscience one should never take action. When a person has reason for believing that an intended act may be evil, he has the duty to remove this vincible ignorance before acting. Otherwise he shows bad will for he intends to perform the act whether it is good or evil. A person in such circumstances should not act. His duty is first of all to clear away the doubt. He must reason about the case, inquire for right principles of action from persons equipped to give such knowledge.

In practical life, however, there are times when doubts cannot be directly solved. What then is to be done? This brings us to the reflex principles that are to be used when certain solutions cannot be directly reached and one is called upon to act.

There are two extreme positions possible in solving a doubt concerning the lawfulness of an act. The first is rigorism which holds that one must have direct certainty that one is not bound by the law in order to favor one's liberty. In other words, when in doubt always hold to the law even when it is more probable that one is free to act otherwise. This is manifestly unreasonable. On the other hand, laxism accepts any reason as an excuse from observing a doubtful law. Laxism is devoid of sufficient reason for favoring liberty over law.

There are two systems for solving practical doubts which are in the main used by moralists in modern times. They are probabilism and equiprobabilism. Probabilism is by far the more common. It was first proposed by Bartholomew Medina, O.P. (1528-1581) who has been followed by a vast number of moralists. The probabilist affirms that in cases of practical doubts relating to the lawfulness of acts it is always lawful to follow the opinion in favor of liberty if the opinion is solidly probable, even though the opinion in favor of the law is itself solidly probable or more probable.

The probabilist argues that a doubtful law does not bind. An uncertain law cannot impose a certain obligation. It is improper that a person be deprived of liberty through a dubious law. A law against whose existence or application one has a solidly probable argument is a doubtful law. Consequently one is free to favor liberty.

Equiprobabilism asserts that when there are conflicting opinions which are equally or almost equally probable, it is lawful to follow the opinion in favor of liberty when the doubt relates to the existence of the law, but if the doubt concerns the cessation of the law, the law continues to bind. Liberty is in possession when there is no evidence that a law has a claim on a person. When the doubt is about the cessation of a law, the law must be obeyed because the law certainly has been imposed. A person must prove that it has ceased. This system was taught by the eminent moralist, St. Alphonsus Liguori (1696-1787).

Equiprobability is not sufficiently practical to serve as a guide in practical doubts. The average person lacks the ability to determine the equality of probable reasons for and against liberty. It often happens that an opinion for liberty may seem to be more probable at one time and less probable at another. Usually a person has to make a decision with a certain conscience without a long drawn out deliberation. A solidly probable opinion suffices. By a solidly probable opinion is meant an opinion that is truly and reasonably probable based on a good argument. One need not search for equal reasons on both sides. One may even have arguments against liberty which are more probable. However, if a solidly probable opinion stands that a law is doubtful, the law does not bind. Dubious, weak, frivolous doubts of course are not solidly probable.

There are cases where reflex principles may not be used in favor of liberty. These are cases where some evil to ourselves or to others will occur which the use of the reflex principles cannot avert. In respect to ourselves this pertains when some grave evil either spiritual or temporal probably will occur. For example, if it is really probable that a person will have deliberate carnal thoughts while reading a certain novel for recreation, one must not read it even if it is more probable that one will not deliberately entertain such thoughts. The safer part must be followed.

When there is danger that a grave spiritual or temporal evil may come to others by one's use of reflex principles, one may not use them. A grocer who knows that a poison has gotten into one of his products for sale may not sell any one of the suspected products because it is more probably free of poison. A jury may not render a verdict of guilty against the accused of murder because circumstantial evidence makes the guilt more probable.

Cases:

1. The penalty for cheating in final exams at a certain college is expulsion. There are probable reasons for believing that a student has cheated. The student, a senior in college, has never been accused of cheating before. Are there sufficient reasons for his expulsion?

2. The Legion of Decency has condemned a movie as morally objectionable. A friend of good moral character has told John that he saw the picture and did not find it to be morally objectionable. John wishes to see the movie. He believes that it is more probable that it will not be an occasion of sin for him. What should he do?

3. A doctor has written a prescription for a gravely sick patient early in the evening. Late that night he wonders whether he has given the right prescription. Possibly he has erred. It is a stormy night and he is fatigued after a long day's work. He cannot check the matter by telephone. May he solve the difficulty by the reflex principle that he ordinarily

gives the right prescription and so he can safely assume that he probably did so in this case?

4. Joan has received a watch as a gift from her boy friend. A reliable friend has told her that her boy friend stole the watch when he was overseas. An equally reliable friend has told her that her boy friend purchased the watch in Germany. What may or must Joan do?

5. A builder doubts whether a minor building regulation is still in effect. He does not have time to contact the civic authority because a sudden decision is required. He seeks advice from two reliable assistants. One tells him the regulation is still in effect. The other tells him that it is defunct because of new construction methods. What may or must he do?

Suggested Reading

St. Thomas Aquinas, *S. Theol.*, P. I, q. 79 aa 12, 13; P. I-II, q. 19 aa 5, 6.

M. Cronin, *Science of Ethics, op. cit.*, Vol. 1, ch. XIV.

F. Connell, *Outlines of Moral Theology* (Milwaukee: Bruce, 1953), pp. 38-48.

Questions

1. Define conscience.
2. Evaluate the rather common belief that conscience is a matter of personal moral sentiment.
3. Analyze the judgment of conscience.
4. What is meant by an antecedent conscience? A consequent conscience?
5. Define a true conscience, an erroneous conscience, a vincibly erroneous conscience, an invincibly erroneous conscience.
6. Define a certain conscience, a doubtful conscience.
7. State and explain the two general principles governing judgments of conscience.
8. Evaluate the popular belief: "Religion is a matter of personal conscience."
9. What is meant by a reflex principle in forming one's conscience? What is rigorism, laxism, equiprobabilism, probabilism?
10. Which system of reflex principles do you adopt? What are the reasons for your choice?

CHAPTER THREE

Obligation and Sanction

I. The Meaning of Obligation.
II. Obligation and Natural Law.
III. The Kantian Ethics of Autonomous Morality.
IV. The Meaning of Sanction.
V. Sanction in This Life and in the Future Life.

I. THE MEANING OF OBLIGATION

MAN IS OBLIGED to keep the law. Law is meaningless unless its subjects are bound to observe it. What is meant by this bond to keep the law? The nature of such a bond is important for the studious inquiry of the ethician. It is especially important in modern times because of the cult of liberty practiced by many, exalting liberty and tending to minimize law and the bond of law. The true notion of obligation is particularly important for us Americans. Some in America are prone to favor personal liberty in the name of human dignity with an overemphasis on the rights of man at the expense of man's obligation to God and His laws in nature. This trend is sometimes evidenced in an extreme reaction to totalitarianism. Reinhold Niebuhr among other Liberals affirmed the view:

> The teachers of totalitarian philosophy have said that everything must be within the state, nothing against the state, nothing outside the state. Democracy teaches that everything must be within humanity, nothing against humanity, nothing outside of humanity.[1]

Let us examine the various ways that one being is bound to another in order that we may appreciate the meaning of the moral bond called "obligation" and come to understand its true source. A being may be bound to something by an external

---

[1] *City of Man* (A Group Statement) (New York: Viking Press, 1940).

physical necessity, by an internal physical necessity or by the moral necessity of a free agent. By external physical necessity is meant the bondage that pertains to slavery, the bondage of force, violence, and coercion such as that existing in the slave state of contemporary Hungary. The subject of such force is the body of man. It does not directly affect the spiritual faculty of the will. The Hungarians are forced to obey the Communist "laws." Freedom from such coercion is called "freedom of spontaneity." It is freedom of spontaneous movement to go, or to come, as the freedom of a man loosed from his chains.

The nature of non-free beings operates with internal physical necessity which binds them to a certain course of action as the nature of fire is to burn, of a plant to vegetate, an animal to act according to its instincts. Freedom from such inner physical necessity is called freedom of choice, liberty of determination, rooted in the spiritual faculty of the rational free will.

As opposed to these bonds of coercion and internal physical necessity there is the moral bond, the moral obligation to act or not to act. This imposes a moral necessity which is distinct in kind from external and internal physical necessity. Moral obligation is a moral necessity in the will arising from the apprehended connection of an act that should be done or omitted in respect to an end to be pursued or avoided.

Freedom from a moral obligation is called freedom of independence. Freedom of speech, freedom of the press, freedom of thought, academic freedom are to be understood in this context. They do not merely connote freedom from force or freedom from internal physical necessity. They signify freedom of independence from the obligation of law in some respect. All such freedom has a restricted meaning within the moral order. Some theorists in America are accustomed to speak of freedom of independence as a kind of absolute. They fail to understand the limits of such moral freedom because they fail to understand moral obligation. A person is not free to teach or speak as he pleases. He is morally obliged to the truth. Hence he may be punished, for example, by the civil authority when his teaching or speaking opposes the common good as inciting to riot, lynchings and other public evils.

The pornographer cannot plead for freedom of the press as

ground for corrupting the public's morals nor can the practical joker who cries "Fire" in a public place be excused because he claims freedom of speech. Moral obligations to the common good restrict personal freedoms.

What is the source of moral obligation? Is it derived from man's own nature or from outside of man? If it has its source outside of man, is it in man's institutions such as the state or is it beyond the human order entirely? Does moral obligation come from God?

From the sixteenth century onwards when a pluralism of religions sprang up in the West some men looked more and more to the state for moral guidance. They were inclined to root moral obligation in the civil law. This is the position of the moral positivists such as the American jurist, Oliver Wendell Holmes.

In the modern era there has been a growing trend among the utilitarians such as British philosopher Jeremy Bentham (1784-1832) to derive moral obligation from man's need to promote social prosperity. Another common modern trend is Kantian humanism which attempts to establish the source of moral obligation in man himself. Moral positivism as well as utilitarianism are closely allied to the Kantian explanation as we shall see.

Moral obligation is in the order of moral necessity rooted in the rational will as was shown. It is really distinct from external or internal physical necessity. Moral necessity arises from the final cause of action since only a good or end known by the intellect can move the will.[2] One cannot will the end without the means for acquiring the end. Morally good human acts are the means to the ultimate end of man, which is God, as was shown. Man's moral obligation is to seek God, his Ultimate End, by means of a good moral life. The source of man's moral obligation is therefore God, his Ultimate End.

Man cannot be indifferent to his ultimate end, his destiny, since this is the reason for his being. Nor can he be indifferent to the means to the end which are determined by his rational nature, as was demonstrated in our study of morality. Every man by moral necessity is bound to seek God by living a morally good life.

---

[2] S. Theol., P. I-II, q. 10, a. 1.

II. OBLIGATION AND NATURAL LAW

God manifests His eternal law to man in its natural content through the natural law which is knowable by reason, as we have seen. Man's natural obligations must therefore be based on what is known through the natural law. Human positive law, the civil law, can bind in conscience only insofar as it is grounded in the natural law. Man-made laws cannot of themselves impose moral obligations because they do not determine the means to man's ultimate end nor the ultimate end itself. A positive law which is determined as a conclusion from the natural law binds in conscience such as laws against murder, theft, bearing false witness.

Does every civil law bind in conscience by reason of the natural law? For example, there is a law against opening a package of cigarettes without breaking the tax seal. Certainly it is not in the mind of the legislator to have this bind in conscience. Such laws which are not conclusions from the natural law but rather are deduced from the natural law as determinations for the common good do not bind in conscience unless they are made to bind in conscience by the legislator for some good reason.[3] For example, one is bound in conscience (for the public safety) to obey traffic regulations.

There are other reasons why a person obeys a law apart from moral obligation, such as for personal advantages which may follow from conforming to law and also because the threat of punishment makes it expedient to obey. However, it should be clear that these are not sufficient reasons for obeying the law and in due time experience manifests their insufficiency. There are circumstances when it is not personally advantageous to obey the law. On the contrary, conformity to law at times can bring hardship and even personal ruin, for example, in military service to the nation in time of war. There are also circumstances when threat of punishment has no real meaning because one can escape punishment. Corruption in government such as bribery of officials sometimes induces a relaxation of penalties or renders them ineffectual. Only moral obligation remains a sufficient reason for obeying the law. A

---

[3] P. N. Zamit, *Philosophia Moralis* (Romae: Angelicum, 1139) Vol. 11, p. 306.

community of morally good citizens is a community ruled by law. Too often law is identified with police action and its motivation is identified with fear of penalty. In the properly realistic sense law is naturally obeyed out of moral obligation, out of love for order, truth, goodness.

III. THE KANTIAN ETHICS OF
AUTONOMOUS MORALITY

A. EXPOSITION: Immanuel Kant may be called the modern philosopher of morals who greatly influenced the trend to ground ethics in man. The subjectivism and relativism of the religious and intellectual environment in which he was reared in eighteenth century Germany contributed greatly to his trend of thought. For Kant the moral law is within; it is rooted in a good will and springs from a natural inclination of duty. In his *Foundations of the Metaphysics of Morals* he sets down the principle that actions done from the motive of duty alone have moral goodness. By duty Kant understands respect for the law.

> ... The pre-eminent good can consist only in the conception of *the law in itself* (which can be present only in a rational being) so far as this conception and not the hoped for effect is the determining ground of the will. This pre-eminent good which we call moral, is already present in the person who acts according to this conception, and we do not have to expect it first in the result.[4]

Hence this respect for law is the respect for law in itself. Kant asserts that in acting we must examine ourselves to see if the principle on which this act rests can be a universal principle binding on all. This is the categorical imperative with which we have already dealt in the chapter on morality. Kant explains:

> There is, therefore, only one categorical imperative. It is: Act only according to that maxim by which you can at the same time will that it should become a universal law.[5]

In our moral lives we should not look for exceptions in ourselves. We should obey the law as others should obey it out

---

[4] I. Kant, *Foundations of the Metaphysics of Morals*, Sec. I.
[5] *Ibid.*, Sec. II.

of duty to law as a pure concept. Kant derives from the moral law the three postulates of ethics: the freedom of the will, the immortality of the soul and the existence of God.

> Granted that the pure moral law inexorably binds every man as a command (not as a rule of prudence), the righteous man may say: I will that there be a God, that my existence in this world be also an existence in a pure world of the understanding outside the system of natural connections (hence free), and finally that my duration be endless. I stand by this and will not give up this belief.[6]

These truths are not hypotheses nor rational convictions for Kant any more than they are for many Protestant thinkers of our times. They are rather demanded to be accepted on belief, which Kant calls "pure rational faith." This is a faith made by an act of man's will or what came to be called a religious sentiment, and later a phenomenon of religious experience.

B. CRITICISM: It is conceded that duty is a legitimate motive for obeying law but denied that duty is the source of moral obligation. Duty is dependent on right. Duty is never self-explanatory. Man has a duty to live morally because man is destined to God, his Ultimate End. God has the supreme right over His creature who must dutifully abide by the moral law in pursuit of his destiny, the Supreme Good. God alone is the source of man's moral obligations as the Ultimate End of man.

The human will is itself a blind faculty. It can only pursue duty because the intellect informs it of duty. The will follows the intellect. The identification of moral obligation with duty established primarily in the will can only lead to sentimentalism, a purely subjective norm of morality. A person of good will has objective moral significance only because his will illumined by the intellect seeks what is objectively good. The formal idealism of Kant, however, prohibited him from mastering a truly objective ethics. God, free will, the immortal soul, good and evil are not merely good subjective notions. They have

---

[6] I. Kant, *Critique of Practical Reason*, P. I, Bk. II, Ch. II, viii.

real significance as the realistic philosophy of Thomism demonstrates in Metaphysics and Rational Psychology.

The moral obligation of Kant's autonomous will is only an obligation in name. The categorical imperative that a person live so that his actions reveal a universal law of action that holds for everyone, cannot morally bind us, if it is merely the product of our own good will. The human will cannot bind itself. It cannot be at the same time superior and inferior, the judge and the judged. St. Thomas asserts: "No one by his own actions imposes a law."[7] "No one properly is coerced by himself."[8] The moral law has moral obligation only from a Supreme Lawgiver or it is a farce.

The contemporary trend to explain moral obligation in the light of man alone apart from God as witnessed in writers such as Albert Camus, Harry Overstreet, Sidney Hook, among others, signifies only confusion. It reduces moral duty to a point of view, a journey in sentiments which varies according to the condition of a person's state of mind and will. Universal moral law has real meaning only in the light of the Universal Good, the Supreme Good in Whom all imperfect goods share in their being.

IV. SANCTION

It is a fact of experience that all people do not abide by their moral obligations. What can the lawgiver do to insure the observance of law? Education in moral principles is not enough. Infractions of the law are not always the result of insufficient training in the true meaning of laws and their contribution to the common good and the individual good of people. Very often the lawbreaker is well aware of the laws of his community and what they mean to public and private welfare. The lawgiver must induce such persons to observe the law by the threat of punishment for breaking the law. Sometimes it is also beneficial for the lawgiver to give rewards as an added inducement to observe the law. The promise of a reward for observing the law and the threat of punishment for breaking it is called sanction.

Sanctions may be considered to have a twofold function.

[7] S. Theol., P. I-II, q. 93, a. 5.
[8] Ibid., q. 96, a. 5.

Firstly in reference to the subjects of the law it induces them to observe the law and it persuades them against breaking it. Secondly in reference to justice sanction seeks to restore the objective order of justice after the law has been observed or broken. Persons who do not abide by the law should not be treated the same as those who keep the law. Justice demands that a person be given his due.

Sanction may be natural or positive. A natural sanction follows from the nature of an act that is done as sickness follows from gluttony or drunkenness. A positive sanction follows by the decree of the lawgiver as a prison sentence is decreed for theft. A sanction is said to be adequate when it gives a sufficient motive for observing the law for the reasonable subject. It is said to be proportionate when it establishes an equality between merit and reward, demerit and punishment. An imperfect sanction is in some way inadequate or unproportioned or both.

V. SANCTION IN THIS LIFE AND
IN THE FUTURE LIFE

Experience testifies that sanctions are imposed by the natural law in this life. A certain harmony does follow in our lives when our human acts conform to their proper ends. A person who lives the good life is especially blest by a good conscience. Peace of mind, health in body, good friendships, honor in the community and a measure of prosperity in the external goods of this world often result from conformity to the proper ends of man in living the morally good life. On the other hand, violations of the natural ends of man often bring to a person trouble in conscience, ill health, evil associations with unfaithful persons and poverty.

Experience also testifies that the sanction of the natural law is not perfect in this life. The good man does not always have health of body, good friends and a measure of prosperity. There are even times when he is troubled in conscience in striving to choose what is right. On the other hand, evil persons sometimes are blest with good health, good friends whom they deceive or who remain faithful to them not withstanding their evil. Evil people are sometimes blest with success and wealth. They may even maintain an untroubled conscience for a good deal of their lives by living a false philosophy. They are often clever enough to escape the sanctions of positive law by deceit, by intrigue, by the aid of capable lawyers, by bribery of civic officials. Evil persons are sometimes not adequately and proportionately sanctioned in this life. For some evils such as suicide there are no sanctions possible in this life.

God, the perfect Lawgiver, cannot be satisfied in His perfect justice by the sanctions of this life. But there must be a sanction given to the natural law because as we have seen reward and punishment are sanctions required for the observance of the law by the just lawgiver. God, Who is the all perfect lawgiver, assigns adequate and proportionate sanctions for the observance of His laws. Since such sanctions are not given in this life and since man is immortal in his spiritual soul, one can naturally expect that sanctions will be given in the life to come.

What is the essential meaning of this sanction imposed by God in the future life? Will it be something of a Mohammedan kind of paradise where the good man will be blest with material welfare? Will the evil man be deprived of the goods of this life as in the fables of the Greeks concerning the Shades beyond the river Styx? The essential meaning of the sanction of the just and unjust must be more than this. It must consist in the attainment of man's ultimate end or its loss for the immortal soul. The just man who has lived according to the means to his ultimate end in the good moral life will attain the ultimate end, the Supreme Good, God, in the life to come. The evil man who has not lived according to the right means by a morally evil life cannot attain his destiny, God. St. Thomas explains:

> But God has imposed upon men's acts an order in respect of their final good. If then that order is duly laid down, it must be that they who walk according to it shall gain their final good, that is, be rewarded, and they who depart from that order by sin shall be shut out from their final good, that is punished.[9]

No other sanction would be sufficient to induce man to observe the natural law. For man is made for God, His Universal Truth and Universal Goodness and Beauty. All else would be an

---

[9] *Contra Gentiles,* Bk. III, Ch. 141.

inadequate sanction short of man's destiny. Other blessings can be given to the just and other evils given to the unjust but they are not what is necessary for an adequate and proportionate sanction for man.

The philosopher can reason to a reward or punishment for man in the life to come in the possession of or privation from the ultimate end, but he cannot arrive at the revealed doctrine of heaven and hell as it is unfolded in the Christian revelation. This is beyond the natural light of reason, although once revealed, reason can attest to its reasonableness.

Suggested Reading

Aristotle, *Nicomachean Ethics*, Bk. VII, ch. 2, 3.
St. Thomas Aquinas, *Summa Theologica*, P. I, q. 82, a. 1 and 2, I-II, q. 10, a. 1 and 2; q. 13, a. 3 and 6.
Contra Gentiles, Bk. III, ch. 10.
M. Cronin, *Science of Ethics, op. cit.*, Vol. I, chs. 8, 9.
N. Farrell, "The Roots of Obligation" in *The Thomist*, Vol. I (1939), pp. 14-30.

Questions

1. Define obligation.
2. Distinguish moral obligation from physical necessity and violence.
3. Compare moral independence as in freedom of speech to moral obligation.
4. What is the source of moral obligation? Prove your reply.
5. Criticize the judgment that moral obligation is always derived from duty.
6. How is moral obligation related to natural law and to civil law?
7. What is meant by sanction?
8. When is sanction adequate and proportionate?
9. Discuss sanction and natural law.
10. What does the philosopher know about sanction and the future life?

CHAPTER FOUR

Merit and Demerit

I. THE MEANING OF MERIT AND DEMERIT

THE CONSIDERATION of merit and demerit, reward and punishment, belongs to the section of ethics concerned with law. Acts that are in accord with the law are meritorious acts; the doer deserves some reward. Acts that are against the law are acts of demerit and they should be punished.

We have seen in the last chapter, that sanction is not always given in this life but in the future life. Sometimes a person is rewarded in this life for a good act or punished for an evil act long after it is committed. For example, a national hero like Columbus was justly rewarded for his discoveries long after they were actually made. Criminals on the other hand are sometimes apprehended years after a crime is committed and finally sentenced to prison. The problem arises as to the relation between an action and its reward and punishment. There must be some moral entity produced in the agent which entitles him to receive a reward or punishment.

This moral entity is called merit. Merit is a right to payment. It is defined as the moral quality in a human act which renders an agent worthy of something. It can designate reward or punishment. It is commonly used to designate worthiness of a reward. A person worthy of punishment for an evil committed by him is said to have a demerit.

Three conditions are required for merit:

1. The act must be physically free. The person must be responsible for what was done; otherwise the act is not imputed to him. Only a person who performs a human act can merit.

A drunkard who accidentally frightens away a burglar is not worthy of a reward.

2. The act must be for the honor or benefit of another. Although the act benefits another, it must not be owed to him by another title or reason. A worker does not merit a bonus, if he is only doing the work for which he is paid his regular salary.

3. The recipient must freely accept the utility. When an employe works overtime without the knowledge of his employer, he cannot claim that the employer owes him for overtime. The acceptance of the utility or favor can be explicit or implicit, by contract, mutual agreement or understood from the customary nature of things.

II. CONDIGN AND CONGRUOUS MERIT AMONG MEN

Merit is generally divided into condign and congruous. A person can merit something out of justice and right or out of decency. Condign merit is merit in the strict sense. It exists when there is an equality between the reward and the act done as, for example, between wages and work performed. A violation of condign merit is a violation of commutative justice and the offender has a consequent obligation of restitution.

Congruous merit is merit by analogy. It exists when the reward is given out of the generosity of the donor, while the intrinsic value of the act done is not proportionate to the reward received. For example, a worker might merit a bonus for work well done by reason of the decency of the employer. Such rewards are gratuities; they are not given out of strict justice. Failure to give such rewards may be called indecent and unfitting but it is not a violation of commutative justice. It may violate gratitude or show some sort of personal discrimination.

The distinction between condign and congruous merit has definite importance in the ethics of human living. People are sometimes apt to confuse merit which is only congruous with what is condign. Favors from persons in political offices or from any superior are sometimes identified with what is owed in justice to a person. Gratuities given by a company to employees sometimes are considered as things owed in strict justice. The generosity of friends is sometimes falsely taken as a good merited not out of the gratuity of friendship but as a duty owed in strict justice.

III. MERIT WITH GOD

Union with man's ultimate end, God, is the reward of the man who has been faithful to the moral law in this life. Our concern as philosophers is restricted to what man can know by reason of natural beatitude and natural merit. The problem with which we are now concerned is precisely how does man merit this reward from God? Is it a matter of justice and therefore condign merit? Or is it a matter of condign merit founded on something other than justice? It is manifest from natural reason that God as the reward of the just man is not merely a matter of congruous merit, that is, something fitting in an accidental way to a person.

Condign merit between God and man cannot be based on justice because, as we have seen in our treatment of justice, justice demands equality of persons. But there is no equality between God and man, Creator and creature. Therefore condign merit between God and man must rest on something other than justice. It rests on God's fidelity to the promise of a reward. Man may know of such a promise from reason, insofar as it pertains to God as the ultimate end of nature. The rational creature can know naturally that the all good God will reward the just with their destiny, the Supreme Good. St. Thomas clearly explains why it cannot be said that this condign merit of a reward from God is a matter of justice.

Now it is clear that between God and man there is the greatest inequality; for they are infinitely apart, and all man's good is from God. Hence there can be no justice of absolute equality between man and God, but only of a certain proportion, inasmuch as both operate after their own manner. Now the manner and measure of human virtue is in man from God. Hence man's merit with God exists only on the presupposition of the divine ordination, so that, namely man obtains from God, as a sort of reward for his operation, what God gave him the power of operation for, even as natural things by their proper movements and operations obtain that to which they were ordained by God. There is a difference, however, since the rational creature moves itself to act by its own free choice and so its action has the character of merit, which is not the case in other creatures.[1]

Hence man can merit from God by his free actions done for God's glory. Man condignly merits a reward from God which is fulfilled by God's fidelity to His promise to reward the creature. This promise in reference to what man can know naturally is implicit in God's ordination of the rational creature to its ultimate end and the means to attain it. It was already proved that the attainment of man's ultimate end is happiness for him and that the means to attain the ultimate end is living the morally good life. An act is not morally good unless it leads man to God and so it cannot be morally good, unless it merits the reward of the felicity of union with God. The creature does not have a right in justice to happiness from God so that God is his debtor. He knows, however, that God has promised him happiness as a reward of the good life and that the all good God is faithful to His promise implicit in the natural movement of man to his ultimate end, the Supreme Good, God. Man's title to happiness is founded on God's gift and promise. It should be clear that our use of the term "merit" in this consideration of merit with God is analogous to its use in reference to merit between men.

Suggested Reading

St. Thomas Aquinas, *Summa Theologica*, P. I-II, q. 114, a. 5; *Contra Gentiles*, BK. IV, Chs. 91-93.

M. Cronin, *Science of Ethics*, Vol. I, pp. 574-584.

J. Sullivan, *General Ethics*, (Worcester: Holy Cross College, 1931), pp. 171-178.

Questions

1. Define merit.
2. State and explain the conditions of merit.
3. What is condign merit, congruous merit?
4. Comment briefly on the popular confusion between what is merited condignly and what is merited congruously.
5. In what sense can we speak of Man meriting something from God? What is the basis for man's meriting something from God?

---

[1] *S. Theol.*, P. I-II, q. 114, a. 1.

CHAPTER FIVE

Crime and Punishment

I. THE MEANING OF PUNISHMENT

ST. THOMAS EXPLAINS that the acts of law are ordained to command, to prohibit, to permit and to punish.[1] The Angelic Doctor distinguishes a threefold order of punishment inflicted on man by himself, by another (for example, the state) and by God.

> Accordingly man can be punished with a threefold punishment corresponding to the three orders to which the human will is subject. In the first place a man's nature is subjected to the order of his reason; secondly it is subjected to the order of another man who governs either in spiritual or temporal matters, as a member either of the state or of the household; thirdly it is subjected to the universal order of the Divine government. Now each of these three orders is disturbed by sin, for the sinner acts against his reason and against human and Divine law. Wherefore he incurs a threefold punishment one, inflicted on himself, viz. remorse of conscience; another, inflicted by man; and a third inflicted by God.[2]

In this chapter our concern is principally with punishment inflicted by the state for crimes committed against its laws. By crime is meant a breach of the public law.

Punishment is payment for demerit. It is defined as any authoritative deprivation of a good in an evildoer in return for an evil committed by him. Punishment belongs to one who has

[1] S. *Theol.*, P. I-II, q. 92, a. 2.
[2] *Ibid.*, q. 87, a. 1.

--◀ 155 ▶--

the authority. Parents may punish their children, the state its citizens, God His creatures. Punishment has for its end the achievement of a good, the maintenance of order. The end of punishment is not the inflicting of evils. A subject may not be punished unless an evil has been committed and the punishment must be proportionate to the evil committed.

II. THE ENDS OF PUNISHMENT:
RETRIBUTIVE, CORRECTIVE AND PREVENTIVE

What are the ends of punishment? In other words what does the authority endeavor to gain by punishment? Punishment in its proper ethical sense refers to the past and to the future. In relation to the past punishment is retributive because it pays back the offender for his crime and strives to establish the equality of justice. It sustains and justifies the law by giving the offender his due. The penal code of a state determines the penalty to fit the crime.

Punishment in relation to the future is corrective preventive. It is corrective because it is directed toward correcting the false ideals of the offender, showing him that crime does not pay and endeavoring to rehabilitate him in the good order of society. It is preventive or deterrent because through the example of the punished offender, it is hoped that others will be deterred from crime. The facts attest that there are persons whose only motive in abstaining from crime is the fear of a prison sentence or capital punishment.[3]

Retribution for crime, the correction and prevention of crime, are not always present in punishment or they are not adequately achieved. The offended party cannot always expect proper retribution. Punishing a criminal for manslaughter cannot restore the life that has been unjustly taken. In respect to the offender capital punishment cannot correct him as a citizen in society. The execution simply removes him as an undesirable, much as one would sever a poisoned limb from the body. Some criminals refuse to be corrected and become more hardened in their odium for right order during their prison term. The percentage of offenders who were in prison previously is a sad

---

[3] George Whitecross Paton, *A Test-Book of Jurisprudence* (Oxford: At The Clarendon Press, 1946) "Theories of Punishment," pp. 346-353.

commentary on the effectiveness of a prison sentence. In the United States the Wickersham Commission writes that it would not be surprised to learn that 60 per cent of the persons received in prison have been in prison before. Although a large percentage of "first-timers" are not convicted again, the probability of relapse increases with the number of previous sentences.[4] In 1940 it was claimed that the present penal methods are successful in 70 per cent of the cases.[5]

It seems that in the majority of modern states the usual legal approach to offenders of the law is utilitarian: the law must protect society,[6] order must be maintained. However, the retributive and corrective elements of punishment are also present. Modern criminology has contributed much toward fitting the penalty to the mental condition of the criminal. Ordinarily, however, the retributive principle that the penalty should fit the crime should not be forsaken. The victim should be considered as well as the criminal. Evildoers must be sanctioned proportionately; unless it is proved that they did not act freely.

III. PUNISHMENT AND THE STATE

Every moral offense is not punishable by the state. St. Thomas explains that the state punishes only certain vices:

> ... human laws do not forbid all vices ... but only the more grievous vices from which it is possible for the majority to abstain and chiefly those that are to the hurt of others without the prohibition of which human society could not be maintained: thus human law prohibits murder, theft and such like things.[7]

The penal code of a state does not provide for punishment in the case of every moral offense but only for the more grievous vices. These are vices from which the majority of citizens can abstain and principally those vices which do damage to another and which offend the public order in some way. Any attempt to enforce an ethical code in its entirety by the criminal law

---

[4] Paton, *op. cit.*, p. 360.
[5] *Ibid.*
[6] *Ibid.*, p. 348.
[7] *S. Theol.*, P. I-II, q. 96, a. 2.

is doomed to failure. This was amply illustrated in the "blue laws" of the early New England colonies. The enforcement of a Puritan code of ethics was attempted by the state.

Private individuals in a community cannot take it upon themselves to punish others for damages inflicted. The rule of law demands that the state be reserved this right. St. Thomas teaches:

> To punish pertains to none but the framer of the law by whose authority the pain is inflicted.[8]

Lynching mobs, the vendetta or feud for blood revenge, and all instances where private individuals appropriate to themselves the rights to punish which belong to the state are wrong. The Ku Klux Klan is perhaps the best known secret society in the United States formed to punish offenders against what its members believe to be the good of society.

The state requires the offender of a damaged party to make restitution for the injury inflicted on another, inasmuch as this is possible. However, even when restitution is made, justice is not satisfied because restitution restores things as they were before the damage was done. The damage precisely as a crime, a breach of the public law, must be paid for. Restitution does not remove the need for punishment for crime.

The thief who breaks into a home and steals the property of another must not only restore the stolen articles or their equivalent in money to the rightful owner inasmuch as this is possible but he must also pay for the crime that he has committed. There would be insufficient sanction given if all the offender had to do would be to make restitution to the offended party. It would be very inviting for the offender to try again at a future time in the hope of escaping the burden of restitution and with no danger to his personal liberty.

It is the duty of the state to punish the criminal with a suitable penalty, to endeavor to reform him from his criminal ways, and to deter others from the ways of crime. The crime, however, as an offense against God remains. Neither the criminal nor the state can adequately satisfy for an offense against divine justice, the infinite majesty of God. God in His providence can either forgive or punish or both according to His justice, wisdom and mercy.

---

[8] S. Theol., P. I-II, q. 92, aa. 2 and 3.

In Russia the Soviet law divides crimes into minor and major. Major crimes strike against the safety of the Communist state. Harsh penalties are given to offenders against the state. Any guarantees to the prisoner of his rights which might conflict with the state are dismissed. Trial by jury is mistrusted because the jury might not give a verdict in accord with state policy. Punishment of the political prisoner is most severe in Russia and her satellites. This system of injustice now dominates one third of the earth's population.

IV. THE FOUNDATION OF RETRIBUTIVE PUNISHMENT

There have been systems of law which neglected the corrective and preventive ends of punishment by overemphasizing its retributive end as if punishment is an end in itself rather than a means to the end of maintaining the common good of society. Such systems narrow punishment to vengeance, an eye for an eye. In the time of George III in England there were as many as 220 capital offenses. Right thinking people were justly aroused against the death penalty for such offenses as cutting down a tree or robbing a rabbit warren. However, it is wrong to assume from such excessive practices that retributive punishment is only and always founded upon vengeance.

Among the ancients Plato opposed retributive punishment as barbaric and considers only the corrective and deterrent aspects of punishment.

> No one punishes the evildoer under the notion, or for the reason, that he has done wrong; only the unreasonable fury of the beast acts in this manner. But he who desires to inflict rational punishment does not retaliate for a past wrong which cannot be undone; he has regard for the future and is desirous that the man who is punished, and he who sees him punished, may be deterred from doing wrong again. He punishes for the sake of prevention.[9]

Recently an article in a popular New York City newspaper repeated this platonic argument in a plea against capital punishment.

> Over the years the death sentence, once a common penalty for any offense from turnip stealing to treason, has been

---

[9] *Protagoras,* 324.

gradually dying. Fourteen Western nations and seven United States states have abolished it entirely. As people learn more of the cause and cure of criminal behavior and as the steady advance of human understanding refines our moral values, execution appears as an ugly anachronism. When the state itself kills deliberately and avoidably, it can speak only with tainted breath in asking that its citizens not kill.

In the modern liberal society a great deal of attention has been given to the cause and cure of crime. Biological, psychological and economic causes have been considered in an effort to correct and prevent crime. The studies of Professor Hooton have empirically established that physical characteristics do not dispose a person to crime.[10] Psychoanalysis has shown that some criminals need hospitalization rather than just a prison sentence. Statistics show that in periods of economic depression the number of crimes increase.

It is impossible to regard crime as the simple result of any one cause. However, there are theorists who attempt to explain crime as the result of some physical factor such as disordered functioning of the ductless glands. Others regard crime as a mental disorder and still others identify it with bad environment due to economic factors. Preoccupation with the correction and prevention of crime has led to the neglect of retributive punishment and the view that it is caused only by irrational vengeance.

An objective philosophy of morality is needed especially in our times to identify the foundation of retributive punishment. The view that ethics is subjective and relative, which is rather wisespread among jurists, causes them to study crime and punishment from biological, psychological and economic aspects rather than from the ethical, legal aspect. The law of course should consider these other aspects as modifiers of human arts.

The essence of retributive punishment is not found in doing evil for evil. It is founded on justice, in giving a person his due. All law must consider justice. The state punishes out of retribution in order to re-establish the balance of justice; otherwise sanction loses its power to protect the law. The just and the unjust would have equality before the law, unless the unjust

---

[10] E. A. Hooton, *Crime and the Man* (Harvard: 1939).

were punished for a crime committed. The law must show that it does not tolerate evildoers.

Retributive punishment can only be administered by the state as opposed to its individual citizens for one reason, because the state is neutral. It does not act out of vengeance as can easily be the case when the offended punishes the offender. Retribution is the primary reason for punishment. If punishment were administered purely for corrective and preventive reasons, a person could be punished before committing a crime. The primary reason for punishment is to be found in the crime itself as committed, which offends the virtue of justice, the foundation of law rooted in the moral nature of man.

Capital punishment has no corrective force for the criminal executed. Its reasons are retributive and preventive. It is reserved for grave crimes against the individual and public good in retribution for establishing the balance of justice and to deter others from grave offenses. Even though a state does not prescribe capital punishment, it has the right to do so in peace and war.

Suggested Reading

Aristotle, *Nicomachean Ethics*, Bk. V. a. 2.

St. Thomas Aquinas, *Summa Theologica*, P. I-II, qq. 87, 92, 96, 108, a. 1.

H. Barnes and W. N. Teeters, *New Horizons in Criminology* (N.Y.: Prentice Hall, 1951).

G. W. Paton, *A Text-Book of Jurisprudence* (Oxford: At The Clarendon Press, 1946) "Criminal Law" pp. 346-373.

Questions

1. What is the threefold order of punishment inflicted on man?

2. Define punishment. (a) Who has the right to punish? (b) When may a person be punished and how is the penalty to be determined?

3. State and define the three ends of punishment. Are these three ends present in every punishment? Explain your reply.

4. What moral offenses are punishable by the state? May private citizens punish offenders of the public order?

5. Distinguish restitution from retributive justice.

6. Can punishment administered by the state satisfy divine justice? Explain your reply.

7. Defend the thesis that retributive punishment is founded upon justice and not vengeance.

8. Criticize the following judgments which plead that punishment

is essentially corrective and preventive and should be nothing more:

a. Criminals are either insane or suffered temporary insanity at the time of their crime. They should be analyzed by psychiatrists rather than punished by the penal system.

b. Crime is caused by environmental factors especially poverty. Social adjustment is the cure for crime rather than the vengeance of punishment.

9. Is capital punishment useless because it cannot correct the executed offender?

10. Why is an objective philosophy of morality important to the jurist for a philosophy of punishment? Should it be abolished because it does not always deter people from committing capital offenses? What is the basic reason for capital punishment?

CHAPTER SIX

Rights and Duties

I. THE MEANING OF RIGHT AND DUTY

Law imposes obligation: Consequently from law arise the rights and duties of man. By laws we do not mean merely the civil law, as if the only rights and duties of man are those written in the statutes of the law of a state. Ultimately all rights and duties arise from the eternal law, proximately from the natural law and the civil law inasmuch as they arise from human needs based on the natural law.[1]

In English the term "right" is used in a variety of ways. It is sometimes used as the equivalent of "law,'" as when it is said: "Natural right to happiness is a basic truth." Right may also signify what is due to a person, as when we say "We demand our rights." In ethics the basic meaning of right concerns a moral power in a person, for example, "Man has a right to a good name."

Right is defined as the moral power to do, to hold or to demand something. It is a moral power and not a physical power. Might is not the same as right. Right is called a moral power because it is a capability of doing, holding or demanding something that arises out of the moral law. Even though a person does not have the physical power to maintain or obtain

---

[1] S. Theol., P. II-II, q. 57, a. 2.

his rights, the rights do not cease to be. The thief who overpowers a man and steals his goods does not thereby possess them rightfully. The thief has the might but not the right.

Right, "a moral power to do something," means that one has the right to perform or omit something, as for example, the right to marry or not to marry. "The right to hold" means the right to own, retain or make use of something as the right to own, retain and use private property. "The right to demand" means the right to exact from another the performance or omission of something. A person may demand that another respect his right of ownership of property.

Right may be subjective or objective. It is considered subjectively when it is related to the person who is the subject of the right, as the rights of a wife, the rights of citizens, the rights of a person in a certain but erroneous conscience. Right is considered as objective in the relation of the right to the thing or object concerned, for example, the right of private property, the right to vote.

In our study of conscience it was said that a person has a subjective right to practice a false religion but not an objective right. There is no objective right in the case inasmuch as there is no object, namely religion, since the religion is false; it lacks objectivity. There is a subjective right in the person to do what he believes is right. The object in his conscience is what he sincerely believes to be a true religion. In this context precisely as a right the subject is the person believing and the object is what he sincerely believes to be a true religion, which in fact is not.

Duty is correlative to right. Duty is the moral obligation to do or omit something. If a person has a right to something, another person has a duty, as the duty to respect that right. If one man has a duty, then another man or God has a right. God alone has rights and no duties to another. Since God has supreme dominion over all, He cannot be subject to the payment of duty to His creatures. Duties as rights arise from law because obligation is founded on law, as was shown in Chapter III of this part of *General Ethics*.

II. THE SUBJECT, TERM, OBJECT AND FOUNDATION OF RIGHT

The subject of a right is always a person who possesses it. The term is the person obliged to fulfill the rights of another. The object is the thing to which one has a right. The title is the reason why a person has a right to something. An employee has a right to a just wage by reason of the service done for an employer. The employee is the subject of the right, the term of the right is the employer; the wages are the object and the services rendered are the title of the right.

Only persons can have rights and duties, because only persons are capable of moral acts as free, rational agents. We sometimes speak of the rights of animals to decent care by man but this is an improper manner of speaking. Man has the duty to care for animals that are his private property and to abstain from any actions which would misuse animals as goods of providence given in the order of nature. One offends natural law by cruelty to animals not because animals have rights but because man has duties to them. Duty presupposes right only among persons.

A person as the subject of right and duty can be an individual person, as Mr. Jones, or a moral person, as a corporation or a state. People can be the subject of rights and duties either individually or in moral union formed for some end. Even though a person by reason of immaturity as a child or by reason of insanity cannot control himself, he is still the subject of certain rights according to natural law, as the right to life, to bodily integrity.

The term of the right must always be a person because only a person can be obliged to fulfill a right as his duty. The matter or object of a right can never be a person. A person is self-owned, he can never be owned as a person by another created person because he is destined for God, his Ultimate End. A husband does not own his wife's person, nor a father a child's person, an employer can never own his employee's person, nor can the state own its citizens as persons. No one can claim another person as his property but one can have a title to their activities in some way. The metaphysical real distinction between a rational being and its activities is important in this context.

The title of a right is the reason for the right. It is the foundation for the right. A man has a title to this parcel of land by reason of the contract of sale. Sometimes a person has a right by reason of his human nature.[2] Such a title is by natural right as the right to life, to liberty, to the pursuit of happiness. A person may also have a title to something by private agreement between individuals or the common consent of men or a state, as when a statute gives to a company a monopoly of the sale of a product, for example, public utilities, as the telephone company. These are called positive rights.[3]

III. SLAVERY AND HUMAN RIGHTS

A slave, as such, belongs to his master; yet each, considered as a man is something having separate existence and distinct from others. Hence insofar as each is a man, there is justice toward them in a certain way. . . .[4]

"A slave as such belongs to his master . . . " These and other citations from the writings of St. Thomas Aquinas might appear to be an approval of slavery by the Angelic Doctor. St. Thomas is speaking of a moderate form of corporeal servitude in which a master has a claim to certain servile works from another regulated by justice. This is to be distinguished from absolute slavery in which a master claims to own the person of the slave as the property of the master. Ordinarily nowadays slavery is taken in this meaning. It is the sort of slavery practiced on some 4 million men, women and children according to a 1950 estimate in Northern Africa, Arabia, Abyssinia, China. There are millions in slave labor camps of the Union of Soviet Socialist Republics and the communes of present day China.

St. Thomas tolerated the mitigated slavery of serfdom in his times because of the prevailing economic conditions. However, he could never endorse slavery in its proper sense or absolute slavery because of the principle: ". . . a man differs from irrational animals in this, that he is master of his actions."[5] A

[2] S. *Theol.*, P. I-II, q. 57, a. 2.
[3] *Ibid.*
[4] *Ibid.*, a. 4, ad 2.
[5] S. *Theol.*, P. I-II, q. 1, a. 1.

person can never be the object of the right of another: to be bought and sold as cattle in the market place. Human dignity does not allow a man to be used as an instrument, as the property of another man. Every man naturally flees from slavery, as he naturally flees from any other evil.[6]

Slavery in any form is adverse to the first intention of nature which is that a man be master of his own acts. Mitigated slavery is not against nature, however, as a punishment for crime. Prisoners are subject to a mitigated form of slavery. They are not free men inasmuch as they are forced to remain in prison and to follow a penitentiary discipline. However, criminals are not absolute slaves. The state can not own their person as its property. Prisoners have certain rights according to justice as the right to adore God, the right to an adequate diet, to ordinary medical care. The duties of servitude are always limited to external activities of the human body. In things pertaining to morality a man is subject to God alone.

> For Seneca says (*De Beneficiis,* iii): "It is wrong to suppose that slavery falls upon the whole man: for the better part of man is excepted. His body is subjected and assigned to his master, but his soul is his own." Consequently in matters touching the internal movement of the will man is not bound to obey his fellow-man but God alone.[7]

IV. NATURAL RIGHTS

Natural rights are rights that follow from natural law. Natural right is not the same as natural law. However, on the eve of the American and French revolutions the concept of natural law had become largely a concept of the natural rights of man. Natural rights became a liberating principle for the use of modern man in his challenge of existing political institutions.[8] In the opening paragraphs of the *Declaration of Independence* of 1776 we read:

> When in the Course of human events, it becomes necessary for one people to dissolve the political bands, which

[6] S. *Theol.,* P. I-II, q. 2, a. 4, ad 3.
[7] *Ibid.,* P. I-II, q. 104, a. 5.
[8] A. d'Entreves, *Natural Law* (London: Hutchinson's University Library, 1952), p. 60.

have connected them with another, and to assume among the powers of the earth, the separate and equal station to which the Laws of Nature and of Nature's God entitle them, a decent respect to the opinions of mankind requires that they declare the causes which impel them to the separation. We hold these truths to be self-evident, that all men are created equal, that they are endowed by their Creator with certain unalienable Rights, that among these are Life, Liberty and the pursuit of Happiness. That to secure these rights, Governments are instituted among men, deriving their just powers from the consent of the governed.

The natural rights of man are founded on the natural law which participates in the eternal law of the Creator. The statutes of positive law of a nation as declaring the rights of men are founded in some way on the natural law. Man is naturally obliged to seek his ultimate end which is happiness, the possession of God. Obligation, however, presupposes the rights to fulfill what is obliged, to have the proper means to the end. Therefore, there are natural rights which are common to all men which follow from the nature of man. The state does not confer these rights nor are they acquired by custom or by any form of contract. They simply belong to man naturally.

St. Thomas explains that a natural right belongs to a man by reason of nature or as a result of nature.

Now this may happen in two ways; first, according as it (nature) is considered absolutely: thus a male by its very nature is commensurate with the female to beget offspring by her, and a parent is commensurate with the offspring to nourish it. Secondly a thing is commensurate naturally with another person, not according as it is considered absolutely, but according to something resultant from it, for instance the possession of private property.[9]

St. Thomas then explains why private property is a natural right as a resultant of nature.

For if a particular piece of land be considered absolutely, it contains no reason why it should belong to one man more than to another, but if it be considered in respect of its adaptability to cultivation and the unmolested use

[9] *S. Theol.*, P. II-II, q. 57, a. 3.

of the land, it has a certain commensuration to be the property of one and not of another man. . . .[10]

The attack on natural rights is a corollary to the attack on natural law. As we have noted in our discussion of natural law there are many in our contemporary society who deny natural law as an objective norm of morality. In its stead they substitute the rights of man in the light of self-interest in economics, the will of the majority in politics and private opinion in moral and religious matters. This spirit of liberalistic individualism makes man his own end and supreme judge of his rights.

According to Jean Jacques Rousseau (1712-1778) society is not natural to man but rather men agreed to live in society. This agreement is called a social contract. Human rights are therefore solely dependent upon man-made agreements. On the contrary, contracts have their binding force only because they are based on natural law. In other words, contracts must conform to the objective norm of right and not merely to what is agreeable to men. Contracts of themselves as agreements between men do not confer rights.

Perhaps the most eminent proponent of the theory that what is right is solely a product of human institution, is the jurist, Oliver Wendell Holmes. Holmes was a great judge, a United States Supreme Court Justice, a champion of free speech, of social reform legislation and an honest man. In his philosophy of law, however, he regards natural law as a myth and considers only the positive law of man as the source of rights. Holmes believes that the man, or men, who have might make right. He wrote in his work entitled: *The Common Law*:

> Just so far as the public force is given a man he has legal right and this right is the same whether his claim is founded in righteousness or iniquity.[11]

For Holmes might is the source of right. On the contrary only some rights employ the use of force but the essence of the right is not in the physical force itself. There are some rights such as the right to gratitude which do not employ force. The rights that may employ force are called coactive,

[10] S. *Theol.*, P. II-II, q. 57, a. 3.
[11] O. W. Holmes, *The Common Law* (Boston: Little Brown & Co., 1938), pp. 213, 214.

such as the right to protect one's life and property against an unjust aggressor. Under normal conditions the coactive rights are exercised by the state in protection of its citizens.

There are circumstances in which the possession of rights does not have practical meaning as to their use without the protection of physical might. However, it would be a false pragmatic conclusion to assert that the physical protection and enforcement of rights is the same as right. Otherwise the weak and infirm could have no rights. There would be no reason therefore for the protection of the weak and infirm, the children, the aged, the sick. The concept of right can only be explained in the moral order, in the order of human acts in pursuit of their proper end. Physical force is right or wrong as it conforms or does not conform to the proper ends of man.

V. DUTY AND THE LIMITATION OF RIGHT

Every human right is limited. It is never absolute. Nothing created can be an end in itself. Only God is the absolute ultimate end as was demonstrated. A human right is always within the order of justice, which restricts right by duty to others. A person has the right of free speech but this is limited by the duty to respect the good name of one's fellow man, and by other duties. A teacher has the right of academic freedom but this is limited by the duty to respect the moral law. One may not teach that vice is a virtue.

Human rights are limited but there are certain rights that a person must always possess. These are called inalienable rights which can never be renounced by a person nor taken away by another. A person has a strict duty to follow them as the inalienable right to serve God, to preserve one's life justly. Alienable rights are rights that one can renounce, if one chooses and which can be taken away by another with authority, such as the right to drive a car, the right to vote. All natural rights are not inalienable. A person may renounce the right to marry as in taking a vow of chastity in the service of God.

Duties are more or less limited which can be seen from their division into affirmative and negative duties. Affirmative duty arises from affirmative laws which command one to do something such as: Honor your parents. Negative duties follow from negative laws such as: Do not perjure yourself. They command one to omit or at least to avoid something. Affirmative duties may imply negative duties such as the duty to obey traffic laws implies that one does not disobey such laws. Affirmative and negative duties oblige in different ways. Affirmative laws impose a lasting obligation but not in the sense that it requires constant fulfillment. Honor your parents does not mean that one must be constantly attentive to them. A negative law, on the other hand, imposes a duty that requires constant fulfillment. One may never do what is forbidden, such as one may never tell a lie, commit a felony, and so forth.

VI. THE CONFLICT OF RIGHTS AND DUTIES
ILLUSTRATION: THE RIGHT TO WORK AND
DUTY TOWARD UNIONISM

The performance of our duties and the execution of our rights from day to day sometimes involves conflicts of one duty with another, or one right with another, or between rights and duties. The father of a family has the duty to direct his household; he also has the duty to his job in a company. Sometimes his work takes him away from his home and for long periods of time. There is a conflict between duty to one's home and duty to one's job at work.

A person has the right to join a labor union. He also has the right to work. There is a conflict of rights in a closed shop, where the worker must join the union or be deprived of his right to work in that shop. A person has a right to life. An intelligence agent is given a suicide pill and told that it is his duty to take it rather than be caught by the enemy and risk the disclosure of top secret plans. There is a conflict here between the right to life and the duty to one's country.

There are certain general principles that can guide one in making the right moral decisions in such conflicts.

The higher right or duty prevails:

1. By reason of the more important person: God before man, parents before children, one's fellow citizens before foreigners.

2. By reason of the more grave law. Natural law precedes

the positive law. Suicide pills cannot be taken because they violate the natural law even though they be commanded by some authority of a state.

3. By reason of the greater common good. The good of the human race has precedence over the good of any one nation.

4. By reason of the more serious matter. A spiritual good of the rational soul takes precedence over a good of the body.

5. By reason of clearer title. Something that is certain precedes what is doubtful. A thing owed in strict justice precedes a gratuity. One is bound to pay a bill to one's debtors before giving a gift to a friend.

6. By reason of closer relationship. The rights of one's wife precede the rights of one's parents, the rights of friends come before strangers.

7. By reason of greater urgency. The duty of a citizen to defend his country against an unjust aggressor precedes his duties to work for his family.

These rules are stated in universal terms. In concrete cases they are sometimes difficult to apply. Prudence is required in guiding a person to choose the more important right or duty. One can never do what is intrinsically wrong. This principle must always be kept in mind in solving the conflict of duties and rights.

One of the most controversial issues in contemporary America is the conflict between a worker's right to work and his duty to join a union.[12] Should a government compel all workers to join labor unions? Or should the government compel the open shop by forbidding labor and management to sign union shop contracts? Eighteen states have done this in the United States. Or should the government do nothing and leave the matter up to a company and union whether or not all the workers must join the union? This latter is the traditional United States policy.

Ethically the problem of a union shop presents the conflict between a worker's right to work and a worker's duty to join a union. In a union shop an employer can of course hire whomever he chooses but every new employee after a certain

[12] J. Cronin, "The Morality of Right-To-Work Laws" in *Proceedings of the Catholic Theological Society of America,* Vol. XII, pp. 193-201.

trial period (usually 30 days) must join the union and must keep paying dues to it. The union shop does mean compulsion of a sort. Sometimes the compulsion is physical. In such instances it is wrong and action should be taken by the government against such abuses of union power. However, this does not enter into the basic problem of the conflict of the worker's right to work and his duty to join a union.

The classic argument against the union shop is "the worker's right to work". In an open shop a worker can keep working without ever becoming a union member. In practice the open shop is often a closed shop to unionized labor. This is another sort of compulsion from management. The history of labor also records that such compulsion from management at times became physical.

There are dangers in the big labor union as well as in big business. But the dangers would be increased by destroying the balance between labor and management. Labor would be made weaker without unionization in the conditions of the open shop. The right to work is at best fostered by the duty of a worker to join a labor union. Abuses in the labor union as shown in current Senatorial investigations do not demonstrate that the labor union is *per se* evil. Rather they show some unions need to be restored to their proper function in the service of workers. Without organization labor would be weakened in its bargaining power for just wage and management would be unduly strengthened.

It is certainly ethical to require union membership as a duty of workers to the more common good of their group. An individual does not have an unconditioned right to work. The good of the working class and the general order of society must be considered. Actually "the right to work law" is misnamed. It imports an undue protection to management and discourages the protection of the rights of the worker through labor organization. It is a conflict between the rights of management and the rights of labor by reason of the circumstances cited.

Suggested Reading

Aristotle, *Nichomachean Ethics*, Bk. V.; *Politics*, Bk. I. ch. 4-7.
St. Thomas Aquinas, *Summa Theologica*, P. II-II, q. 57, q. 104, a. 5.

M. Cronin, *Science of Ethics* (Dublin: Gill and Son, 1930) pp. 211-255; 660-686.

H. Romnen, *The Natural Law* (St. Louis: Herder Co., 1948) Ch. XII.

J. Maritain, *The Rights of Man and Natural Law* (N.Y.: Scribners & Sons, 1947).

Questions

1. What are the various meanings of the term "Right"?
2. Define right. Explain the terms of the definition.
3. What is meant by subjective and objective right?
4. Define duty. Relate duty to right.
5. What is meant by the subject, object, term and foundation of right?
6. Is right restricted to persons? Explain your reply.
7. Can a person be the object of a right? Explain your reply.
8. What are some ways in which a person has a title to a thing?
9. Distinguish absolute and modified slavery.
   a. Is absolute slavery ever permitted?
   b. Is modified slavery always wrong? Explain your replies.
10. What is a natural right?
    a. Give some examples of natural rights.
    b. What are the two ways that a man can have a natural right to something according to St. Thomas?
11. Discuss liberalistic individualism and natural law. In particular criticize the contractual theory of rights of Jean Jacques Rousseau.
12. What was Oliver Wendell Holmes' theory of right? Criticize his theory.
13. Can a created right be absolute? Explain your reply.
14. Define and illustrate an alienable right, an inalienable right.
15. What is an affirmative duty, a negative duty? What sort of obligation do they impose respectively?
16. What is the problem of the conflict of rights and duties? Give the seven rules toward solving the conflict.
17. Discuss the conflict of right to work and duty to join unions. What is your ethical solution to this conflict?

CONCLUSION

S T. THOMAS' classical treatise *On Law* was written as a part of the *Summa Theologica* at the home of legal science, the medieval city of Bologna. There is no tract among the ancients, even the Institutes of Gaius and Justinian, that compares with the synthesis of St. Thomas' work. He proceeds with a clear, objective concept of law as the ordination of reason promulgated by the person in authority for the good of the community. He then divides law into eternal law, natural law and positive law, and considers each according to the definition of law, and with a balance of judgment that respects the ultimate completion of eternal law and the limits of the natural and the positive law.

Law for Aquinas belongs to the study of morality rather than to politics. There is a danger in Plato's *Republic* and even in Aristotle of studying law and the virtues, rights and duties as directed to the civic life.[1] In this viewpoint ethics can become subordinate to politics. One encounters this same danger in some contemporary trends in education which treat of law, virtue, rights and duties as only social values productive of the good citizen in the community. For St. Thomas law is a way of guiding men toward their ultimate good. The virtuous life leads to God.

The directive and obligatory influence of law traces back to the eternal law, the great plan of the world rooted in God's wisdom. All laws are derived from the eternal law. In man because of his rational will the eternal law is fulfilled with knowledge of the end, and free and conscious pursuit of it. This participation of rational nature in the divine law is called natural law. It is promulgated in man in the development of reason. Positive law in the law of nations and in civil law is derived from the natural law by human reason seeking the ordered pursuit of its proper ends. Conscience applies the moral principles of law to a person's individual actions.

Within the grand order of this synthesis the role of reason

[1] *S. Theol.*, P. II-II, q. 161, a. 1, ad 5.

is respected without making reason the creator of law. The intellect for Aquinas is the faculty of being and unity. Morality is founded in the human being and discovered by reason in the natural inclinations and first practical principles of human nature. The ethics of Aquinas is an insight into man naturally a moral being. In Kant and in many moderns reason is a moral standard of itself alone and law is discovered only in reason. For Kant the goodness of a thing depends on the will and a good will is the only absolute good. All other goods are relative to situations in life. For St. Thomas a human act is morally good because it conforms to the proper ends of human nature and ultimately to the Supreme Good.

The true understanding of sanction which is the reward for conforming to law and punishment for breaking the law, the true concepts of merit and demerit, right and duty depend upon the true understanding of the more basic principles of the meaning of law, morality and human destiny. If our society today tends more toward considering the criminal than the victim, if individuals and various associations within society consider more their rights rather than their duties, if there is too much talk at conference tables about good will rather than good actions ordered to proper goals, these are practical results of a situational ethics. Situational ethics arises from a voluntarism that fails to harmonize happiness, morality and law because it eschews reason and considers human goods subjectively as values that appeal to a person's good will in a given situation.

In America today we are largely victims of a situational ethics that exaggerates the rights of personal freedom and fails to consider adequately the correlative duties, the price to be paid for freedom. There is an overemphasis on bigness rather than true science of and practice in directing technical skills in the moral life of man. There is much talk about control of the atomic weapons but too little thought about the moral control of man who invents, manufactures and uses these weapons.

The plaintive cry of the humanist is heard in the land. Archibald MacLeish in his popular play *J. B.* in his final message proclaims:

The candles in churches are out
The lights have gone out in the sky.
Blow on the coal of the heart
And we'll see by and by.

Amidst the gathering gloom of disasters the humanist puts his trust in man alone rather than God, to solve the human problem by the human love of life. This sort of humanism is indeed the death of the genuine love of mankind because it rejects Love Itself Who is God.

The problem of the reconciliation of law, morality and happiness is unanswered in the minds of many. The Thomistic synthesis provides the answer in the light of natural reason. It provides an objective understanding of human nature and the dignity of man, subject to God in his being, his powers, his activities.

Moral theology builds upon this natural foundation in instructing man in his authentic vocation in the supernatural life in the Life of all the living, in Wisdom Incarnate, Who alone can say "I am the Way, the Truth and the Life."[2] May today's youth more generously respond to the vocation of the truly happy life.

---

[2] John 14:6.

Index of Names

Index of Subjects

3269